Harbin

Shenyang

Beijing ★

Taiyuan

Zhengzhou

Shanghai

Wuhan

Nanchang

Changsha

Taiwan

Guangzhou

Nanning

Published by Science Press, Beijing

Distributed by Van Nostrand Reinhold Company

    New York, Cincinnati, Toronto, London, Melbourne

Printed in Hong Kong

First published 1980

ISBN 0-442-20013-7

Science Press Book No. 1928-1

中國古人類画集

ATLAS OF PRIMITIVE MAN IN CHINA

Compiling Group of the Atlas,

Institute of Vertebrate Paleontology and Paleoanthropology,

Chinese Academy of Sciences

SCIENCE PRESS

Beijing, China 1980

Distributed by Van Nostrand Reinhold Company

New York Cincinnati Toronto London Melbourne

PREFACE

China is a vast and beautiful land with fabulous resources and a very long history. From time immemorial, ancestors of the Chinese nation have lived, labored and multiplied on this land. This is evidenced by the numerous fossils of early man and the abundance of cultural relics of the Paleolithic Age discovered in China.

Paleoanthropology, the science that studies the evolution of the morphology and distribution of primitive man as well as the development of paleolithic culture, provides basic material data for the study of the history of primitive society.

In the semi-feudal and semi-colonial old China, paleoanthropological studies were severely handicapped and very few fossil sites of primitive man were found. The study of the world-renowned Peking Man fossil remains discovered in Zhoukoudian (Choukoutien), was carried out exclusively by foreign scientists while Chinese anthropologists were denied access. All the priceless Peking Man and Upper Cave Man fossil remains found at Zhoukoudian were trusted to some Americans then working at Peking Union Medical College and were lost about the time of the Pearl Harbor attack in 1941. The whereabouts of the remains are still unknown. Paleoanthropology in China, owing to the gross negligence of its rulers, was practically non-existent from the outbreak of the War of Resistance against Japanese Aggression in 1937 to the liberation of Beijing (Peking) in 1948. The excavation of Longgushan Hill at Zhoukoudian came to a standstill. During this period, neither a single human fossil nor a single stone artifact of paleolithic period was found in China.

In 1949, shortly after the liberation of Beijing (Peking), the excavation and study of the Peking Man site were resumed, and specialized research institutes were established. Sites of Peking Man and Dingcun (Tingtsun) Man were included by the State Council among the first group of major national historical and cultural relics to be protected by the state. In the years since the founding of the People's Republic, remarkable successes have been achieved. While only one ape-man fossil site (at Zhoukoudian) was found in China before liberation, six sites containing hominid fossil remains, contemporaneous with or even earlier than the Zhoukoudian site, have been found north and south of the Changjiang (Yangtze) River, the northernmost site reaching approximately 41 degrees north latitude. Primitive human fossils and paleolithic cultural relics of various subsequent stages were found spread over the country beyond 52 degrees north latitude.

The discovery of Yuanmou Man fossil remains and their dating showed that the primitive man lived more than one million years earlier in China than had previously been supposed. The discovery of human fossil and cultural remains from Maba, Changyang, Tongzi and Dingcun, studies of Gezidong (Pigeon Cave) of Kazuo County, Liaoning Province, and a reappraisal of the stone implements at Locality 15 of Zhoukoudian have contributed to filling in the link in the development from the Protoanthropic man to the Neoanthropic man. The discovery of human fossils from Liujiang, Ziyang, Xujiayao, Shiyu and the studies of the abundant cultural relics of their respective periods have linked the various basic stages of paleoanthropological development more closely and thrown more light on the origin and development of paleolithic culture. Moreover, they provide valuable data for investigations into the formation of modern races and the classification of culture types. The discovery of paleolithic stone artifacts at Dingri in Xizang (Tibet) gives us an insight into the activities of the primitive man on "the roof of the world."

Since 1955, fossil remains of *Gigantopithecus blacki, Dryopithecus keiyuanensis, Australopithecus* sp. and *Ramapithecus lufengensis* have been discovered consecutively in strata in South China, thus giving important clues to research into the origin of man and the evolution of the ape. China is the first find site of *Gigantopithecus* fossils and has been the most productive in the world so far. A very opportune find was the recovery of the first relatively complete lower jawbone fossil of *Ramapithecus* among the considerable number of fossil remains of other animals recovered in the Pliocene stratum at Lufeng County, Yunnan Province.

The locating and study of the Peking Man site have been of epoch-making significance to paleoanthropology. The fact that the ape-man fossils, paleolithic stone artifacts and traces of the use of fire appeared in the same layers of the site has profoundly modified the record of the use of fire by man, making it hundreds of thousands of years earlier than was previously thought. Of greater importance is the proof that Peking Man was a tool-making primitive man. The long-standing controversy over whether the Pithecanthropus of Java was ape-man or man-ape has, in the main, been settled and the existence of the stage of ape-man confirmed. New advances in paleoanthropological studies in China have also contributed to the study of paleolithic culture in Southeast Asia.

The development of productive forces in primitive human society first found expression in the improvement of tools. With the steady improvement of tools, paleolithic implements became fixed in type, smaller in size, more diverse and complex in manufacturing, and corresponding changes and developments were brought about in other aspects. At the same time, there were changes in man's physique. As a result, the primitive man gained more and more freedom and the advance of primitive society was accelerated. *Atlas of Primitive Man in China* illustrates the decisive role of labor in the evolution of man. Labor started with tool manufacturing. Labor created culture. And, in a sense, labor created man.

Although the fossil remains of man and the paleolithic stone artifacts discovered in China belong to various stages, they display many similarities as well as distinct hereditary traits. For instance, the hominid fossils of different stages have similar shovel-shaped incisors, most of the stone implements are back-trimmed on one face and the assemblages of tools are distinguished by the predominance of scrapers over points and choppers. These facts contradict the claims sometimes made that Chinese culture originated in the West.

The *Atlas* is in four parts, with most of the 287 plates in color, dealing respectively with: the Protoanthropic men, the Paleoanthropic men, the Neoanthropic men and the fossil apes. It presents a broad picture of the human fossils and paleolithic stone artifacts discovered in China over the past 50 years, especially the recent achievements in paleoanthropology in China. It is a scientific pictorial atlas about paleoanthropology. To make it easier for the reader to follow the sequence of the early development of man, this book uses the well-known classification: the stages of the Protoanthropic, the Paleoanthropic and the Neoanthropic, each stage provided with brief explanatory notes. Within each stage the sites where relics were found are arranged according to their localities, with due consideration to their chronological order. Moreover, a special section covering briefly the new achievements in the study of fossil apes is included so as to further the reader's understanding of both the transition stage from ape to man and the evolution of the apes.

PROTOANTHROPIC STAGE

The Protoanthropic stage began at the beginning of Quaternary period and ended in the middle Pleistocene period, a span covering about 2,000,000 years. The primitive man in this stage displayed manlike features and retained in the skull morphological apelike characteristics. The skull was rather low, with the broadest part over the auditory orifices. The thickness of the skull might be double that of modern man. It had heavily built brow ridges and a receding forehead. The lower jawbone was heavy and the mouth jutting. It had no chin. The teeth were strong, the molars presenting complicated wrinkles on the occlusal surfaces.

The tools used by the ape-man were simple crude stone tools—choppers, scrapers, points, a few burins and bolli (stone balls). The scrapers were mostly made of stone flakes; flaking included hammer flaking, bipolar flaking and stone-on-stone flaking. Within the Protoanthropic stage there was an increase both in the varieties of stone tools and in the techniques of making them; the shapes of stone tools gradually became more or less uniform.

The mammalian fauna then were markedly different from those of today, with 60 per cent or at least more than 40 per cent of the species now extinct. Some species of the Tertiary period persisted into the early Protoanthropic stage and eventually almost died out by the end of this stage.

Yuanmou Man

On a mound northwest of Shangnabang Village, Yuanmou County, Yunnan Province, geologists found two human fossil incisors on May 1, 1965. The teeth were identified as those belonging to the Protoanthropic stage.

The Yuanmou Man fossil site is the first Protoanthropic site found in South China, and provides valuable clues to the search for ape-man fossil remains and cultures in South China, especially in Yunnan, Guizhou and Sichuan. Its value to the study of the geographical distribution of ape-man fossil remains and his morphological development was noted. In view of the significance of Yuanmou Man in science extensive research was carried out by the institutions concerned. In 1967 and from 1971 to 1975, several excavations conducted at and around this fossil site yielded a large number of mammalian fossils along with three scrapers.

Yuanmou Man lived, as paleogeomagnetic dating indicates, 1,700,000 ± 100,000 years ago. Faunal and floral studies show that a cool climate once prevailed in the region, producing woody plants such as pines, China firs, alders, birches and elms. *Equus yunnanensis, Nestoritherium, Procapreolus stenos, Rusa* and some species of ancient *Muntiacus* inhabited this prairie-forest region.

Incisors of Yuanmo Man. (11.4 mm, 11.3 mm) (E101°55′, N25°45′)

Excavating Yuanmo Man site.

Scrapers of Yuanmo Man. (42 mm, 43 mm, 48 mm)

6

A distant view of Yuanmo Man site.

Skull of *Equus yunnanensis* (Yunnan horse) found at Yuanmo Man site
(basal view). (572 mm)

Antler of *Paracervulus attenuatus* (small deer) found at
Yuanmo Man site. (67 mm)

Maxilla (upper jaw bone) of *Canis yuanmoensis* (Yuanmo
wolf) found at Yuanmo Man site (basal view). (133 mm)

Lantian Man

Lantian Man was found in Lantian County, southeast of the ancient capital, Xi'an. On July 19, 1963, a human lower jawbone was found in the reddish clayey soil near Chenjiawo Village, ten kilometers northwest of the county seat. The jawbone was identified as belonging to an aged female. In 1964 in a similar stratum in Gongwangling, twenty kilometers east of the county seat, the skull-cap of a female of about thirty years old was found. The finds were given the name of "Lantian Man".

In spite of the many morphological affinities of Lantian Man with Peking Man, Lantian Man retained certain features which were more primitive than the latter. It is estimated, for example, that the mean cranial capacity of Lantian Man was 700 c.c. as against Peking Man's 915—1,225 c.c. Comparative studies of the faunal fossils found at the two sites also helped to establish the conclusion that Lantian Man lived 600,000—700,000 years ago, a little earlier than Peking Man.

Near the fossil site of Lantian Man were found fragments of stone tools, mainly scrapers and choppers, and a few proto-handaxes. They are believed to have been made by Lantian Man.

Fossil remains of 38 species of mammals have been recovered, such as *Megamacaca lantianensis* (giant monkey), *Ailuropoda melanolenca* (giant panda), *Megantereon lantianensis* (sabre-toothed cat), *Leptobos* (bison), *Equus sanmeniensis* (horse), *Sus lydekkeri* (pig), *Rusa* (deer). The fauna included some species of mammals of the Quaternary period in South China.

The discovery of Lantian Man is considered a major find in Chinese paleoanthropology after the country's liberation.

Mandible (lower jaw bone) of Lantian Man found near Chenjiawo Village (anterio-lateral view). (E109°20′, N34°10′)

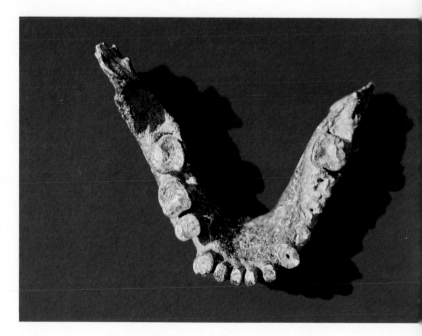

Mandible of Lantian Man found near Chenjiawo Village (occlusal view). (79 mm)

Skull-cap of Lantian Man found at Gongwangling Hill (anterio-lateral view). (E109°30′, N34°10′)

Skull of Lantian Man found at Gongwangling Hill (top view). (134.3 mm)

A distant view of the Gongwangling Hill.

The site where the fossils of Lantian Man were found.

Reconstructed skull of Lantian Man.

A reconstruction of Lantian Man.

Big point of Lantian Man. (186 mm)

Scrapers of Lantian Man.
(49 mm, 37 mm, 46 mm)

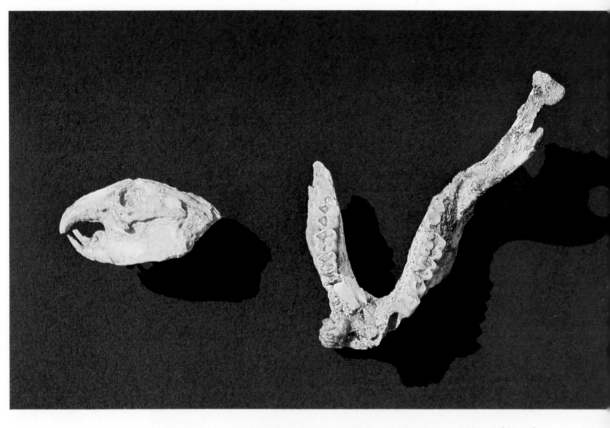

Ochotonoides complicidens (short-ear rabbit) (left) and Megamacaca lantianensis (giant monkey) (right) found at Lantian Man site. (59 mm, 102 mm)

◁Lantian Man mandible site, profile with the three Red Stripes near Chenjiawo Village.

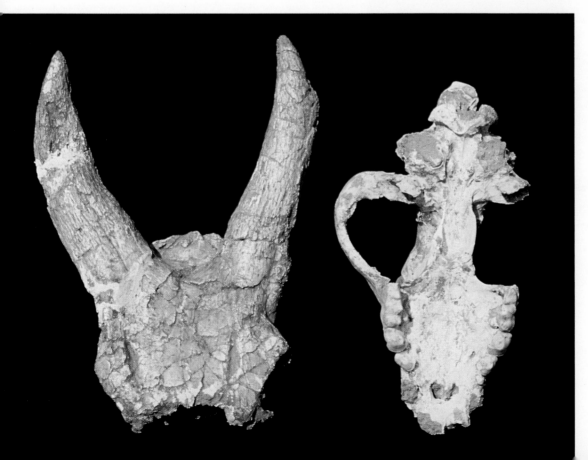

Leptobos brevicornis (bison) (left) and Hyaena sinensis (right) found at Lantian Man site. (210 mm, 350 mm)

Guanyindong Cave, Qianxi

Guanyingdong Cave is an important site yielding cultural relics of early Paleolithic Age in China. The cave was discovered in the winter of 1964, in Qianxi County, Guizhou Province, and three excavations were carried out in 1965, 1972 and 1973. The excavations yielded more than 2,000 paleolithic stone artifacts and fossil remains of some 20 species of mammals from the upper South China red clay stratum and the lower breccia respectively. The stone artifacts unearthed shared characteristics of the early paleolithic stone artifacts found elsewhere in China. For instance, they were mostly flake tools showing traces of back trimming on one face, scrapers predominated over choppers and points and there were not many burins. These stone artifacts also possessed peculiar features of their own: they were not simple stone flakes, they had serrated cutting edges and showed traces of complex retouching as well as vertical or near vertical trimming technique in manufacture. These characteristics necessitated giving a name to this particular culture: "Guanyingdong Cave Culture".

This site yielded fossil remains of more than 20 species of symbiotic mammals. Among them were *Mastoden*, *Stegodon* (elephant), *Rhinoceros sinensis*, *Ailuropoda* (giant panda) and *Crocuta ultima*. The fauna indicated that in the middle Pleistocene period this region was covered with dense forests and prairies, the climate was warm and humid, a landscape entirely different from that of today.

According to the evidence, the Guanyingdong Cave Culture was approximately contemporaneous with that of Peking Man.

Guanyindong Cave—a Paleolithic site in Qiansi County. (E105°55′, N26°55′)

Choppers from Guanyin-
dong Cave. (112 mm,
100 mm)

Scrapers from Guanyin-
dong Cave. (96 mm, 73
mm, 85 mm)

17

Points from Guanyindong Cave. (92 mm, 41 mm, 81 mm, 100 mm)

Maxilla (upper jaw bone) of *Rhinoceros sinensis* (basal view) from Guanyindong Cave. (121 mm)

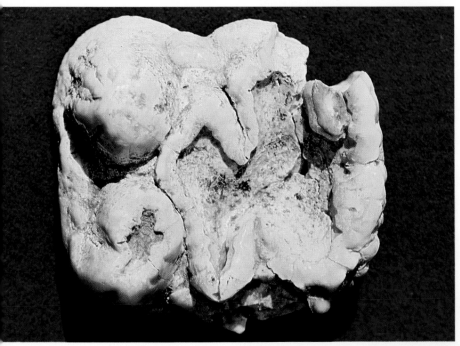

Molar of Gomphotheriidae (mastodon) (occlusal view) from Guanyindong Cave. (88 mm)

Molar of *Stegodon quizhouensis* (elephant) (occlusal view) from Guanyindong Cave. (202 mm)

Yun Xian Man

Teeth of Yun Xian Man. (13.9 mm, 12.6 mm, 10.1 mm)
(E110°57′, N32°58′)

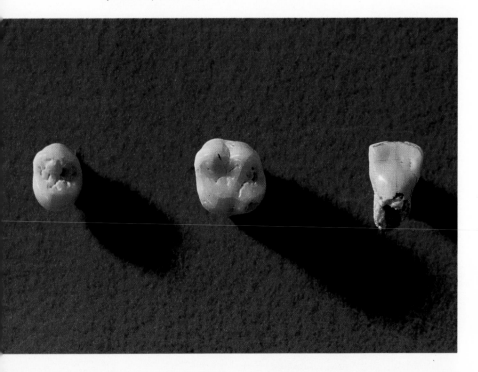

In April 1975, a paleontologist from the Institute of Vertebrate Paleontology and Paleoanthropology turned up with a human incisor fossil from the home of a member of the Meipu People's Commune in Yun Xian County, Hubei Province. This valuable clue led to the discovery of a fossil-bearing site called Longgudong Cave. Excavations of the cave, carried on from May to July and from September to December in 1975, produced two human teeth as well as mammalian fossil remains from the yellowish sandy soil. Preliminary studies suggest that the three teeth belonged to a Protoanthropic man who was thus assigned the name of "Yun Xian Man".

During excavations a stone core bearing clear traces of being worked and fossil remains of more than 20 species of mammals, such as *Hyaena licenti, Sus xiaozhu* (small pig), *Gomphotherium* (mastodon) and *Lutra* (common otter) were found. These major finds are still under study. Preliminary estimates place Yun Xian Man contemporaneous with or slightly earlier than Peking Man.

Teeth of Yun Xian Man (side view).

Excavating Yun Xian Man Cave.

Stone core of Yun Xian Man. (104 mm)

Sus xiaozhu (small pig) from Yun Xian Man Cave. (49 mm)

Hyaena licenti from Yun Xian Man Cave. (129 mm)

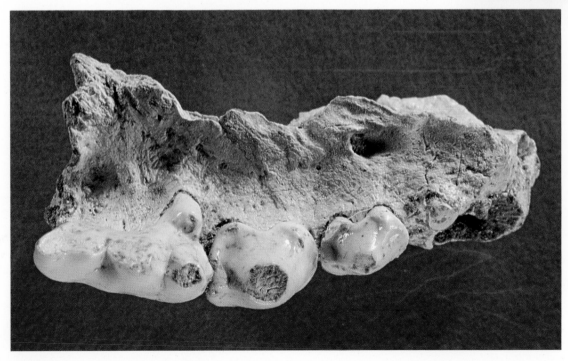

Yunxi Man

Not far from Yun Xian County, another fossil site was found in Yunxi County, also in Yunyang Prefecture, Hubei Province. Fifteen kilometers east of the county seat of Yunxi is Bailongdong Cave on the eastern slope of Shenwuling Hill. In July 1976, the county cultural authorities gathered together all the fossils the people nearby had collected from this cave after heavy rains and discovered among them two ape-man teeth fossils. Further investigation established the site of the fossil teeth and confirmed that they had once been in a light brownish clayey layer in the middle of a deposit inside Beilongdong Cave. The layer is rich in fossils. Fossil remains of more than 20 species of mammals have been found there, such as *Rhizomys* (bamboo rat), *Megantereon* (sabre-toothed cat), *Cervus* sp. (deer) and *Bovinae* (bison). Yunxi Man is estimated to have lived slightly later than Yun Xian Man and at about the same time as Peking Man.

A distant view of Yunxi Man Cave. (E110°45′, N32°58′)

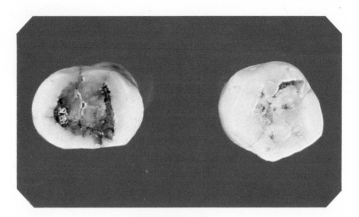

Teeth of Yunxi Man (occlusal view). (11.1 mm, 9.8 mm)

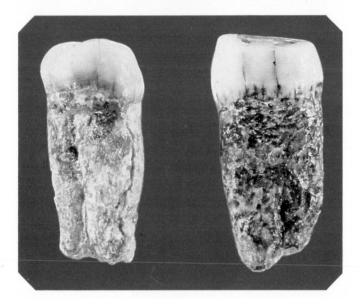

Teeth of Yunxi Man (side view).

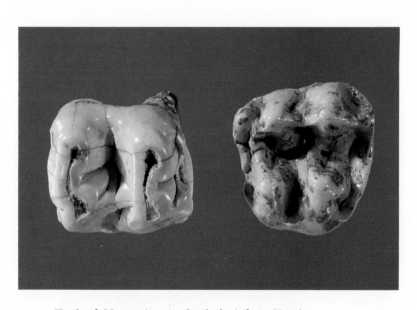

Teeth of *Megatapirus* (occlusal view) from Yunxi
Man Cave. (27 mm, 30.5 mm)

Incisors of *Megantereon* (sabre-toothed cat) from
Yunxi Man Cave. (37.2 mm, 47.3 mm)

Shilongtou Cave, Daye County

This fossil-bearing site of the early Paleolithic Age was found in the winter of 1971 when a water conservancy project was being carried out at Daye Lake, Hubei Province. Two excavations brought to light 88 paleolithic stone artifacts and fossil remains of 11 mammalian species.

The flakes and cores are irregularly shaped, mostly with natural striking platforms. Hammer flaking seems to have been the primary working technique but occasionally there are traces of bipolar flaking. The implements are crude and the edges uneven with many notches. Most of the implements are choppers, with some scrapers.

The animal fossil remains are rather fragmentary. Eleven species have been identified, such as *Ailuropoda* (giant panda), *Stegodon orientalis* (elephant), *Rhinoceros sinensis,* and *Hyaena sinensis,* a species rarely found in South China, but considered typical of the middle Pleistocene epoch in North China. The characteristics of the stone implements and evidence provided by animal fossils set the date of the fossil site as roughly the early Paleolithic Age.

Choppers from Shilongtou site, Daye County. (104 mm, 118 mm) (E115°05′, N30°05′)

Chopper and scrapers from Shilongtou site. (151 mm, 69 mm, 46 mm)

Hyaena sinensis from Shilongtou site (lateral view). (30 mm)

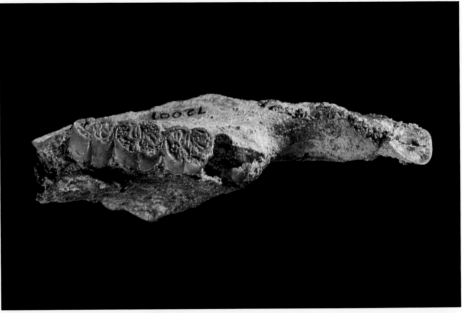

Mandible (lower jaw bone) of *Hystrix* (porcupine) from Shilongtou site (occlusal view). (76 mm)

Shanxi-Shaanxi-Henan

After liberation, extensive archeological investigations were carried out in the area bordering the provinces of Shanxi, Shaanxi and Henan in conjunction with the Sanmenxia Water Conservancy Project. Some fragmentary paleolithic stone artifacts were found in strata of the middle Pleistocene epoch. At Kehe and Nanhaiyu where excavations were conducted, fossil remains of symbiotic mammals were unearthed in addition to stone implements. These helped date the strata.

The paleolithic stone artifacts recovered in the area, mostly flakes and cores, were rather primitive. Stone core choppers predominated. With a few exceptions, the choppers were heavy and crudely fashioned. Small numbers of scrapers and points, crudely manufactured for the most part, were discovered at some localities. Those found at the sites of Kehe and Nanhaiyu were less crude than the others. All these stone artifacts are tentatively placed in the early Paleolithic Age. More accurate classification awaits further studies.

A distant view of Kehe site in Ruicheng County, Shanxi Province. (E110°20′, N34°40′)

Kehe

Stone artifacts from Kehe site. (46 mm, 61 mm, 91 mm, 54 mm)

Mandible (lower jaw bone) of *Megaloceros pachyosteus* (thick-jawbone deer) from Kehe site (occlusal view). (133 mm)

Molar of *Stegodon chiai* (elephant) (occlusal view) from Kehe site. (318 mm)

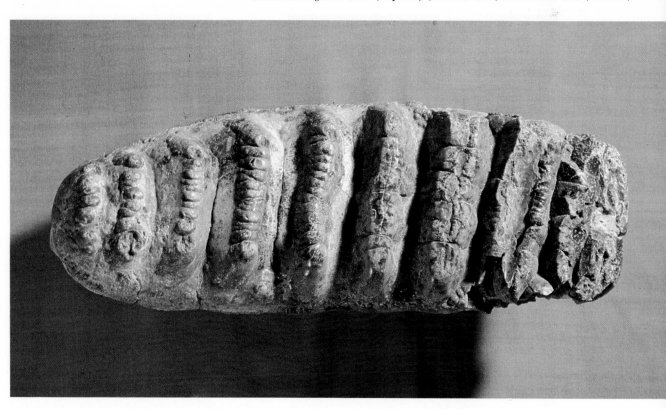

Choppers from Sanmenxia, Henan Province. (177 mm, 131 mm)
(E111°15′, N34°45′)

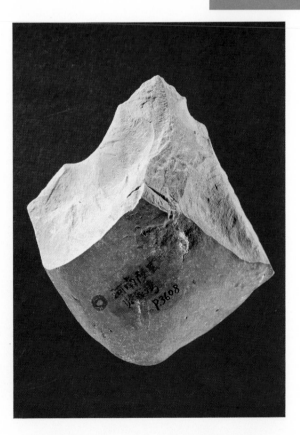

30

Chopper from Zhangjiawan, Tongguan
County, Shaanxi Province. (146 mm)
(E110°20′, N34°35′)

Chopper from Zhangjiawan, Shaan Xian
County, Henan Province. (100 mm)
(E111°15′, N34°45′)

Chopper from Henancun Village, Yuanqu County, Shanxi Province. (164 mm) (E111°40′, N35°20′)

Stone tools from Nanhaiyu, Yuanqu County, Shanxi Province. (59 mm, 45 mm) (E111°40′, N35°20′)

31

Peking Man

Reconstruction of Peking Man (*Homo erectus pekinensis*).
(E115°55′, N39°40′)

At Zhoukoudian not far from Beijing (Peking) proper, a community of ape-men inhabited a cave for a considerable period of time. The cave measures 140 meters in length, from east to west and up to 40 meters in breadth, from north to south. This is now the famous site of Peking Man. Traces of human activities were found in a layer more than 30 meters thick. This layer has yielded 6 skull-caps, 15 lower-jawbones, 153 teeth, 7 fragments of thighbone, 3 fragments of upper arm bones, one fragment of shin bone, one fragment of collar bone, one fragment of lunate (wrist) bone and several facial bone fragments. These bones were ascertained to have belonged to more than 40 Peking Man individuals, male and female, young and old. Several ash layers, meters thick, were found, which contained a large number of charred bones, charred stones and charred hackberry seeds (*Celtis sinensis*). Some 20,000 paleolithic stone artifacts were recovered. In addition to the many hammered and bipolar flakes and cores of various shapes, there was a rich variety of secondary worked stone artifacts—scrapers, points and choppers, and also a few burins and stone balls. The large quantity of human fossil remains, the abundant traces of the use of fire and the wealth of stone artifacts make the home of Peking Man unique among early human fossil sites in the world. It is a veritable treasure-trove of man's early culture.

Vast changes have taken place about this site since liberation. On Longgushan Hill today stands the Peking Man Site Museum, surrounded by trees. The old habitation of Peking Man has turned into a new look. An exhibition center disseminating knowledge about the history of social development, this site attracts a stream of visitors from all over the world.

Peking Man site (inside view).

Dragon Bone Hill with Peking Man site in the center.

Teeth and limb bones of Peking Man found since 1949. (incisor 30 mm, humerus 83 mm)

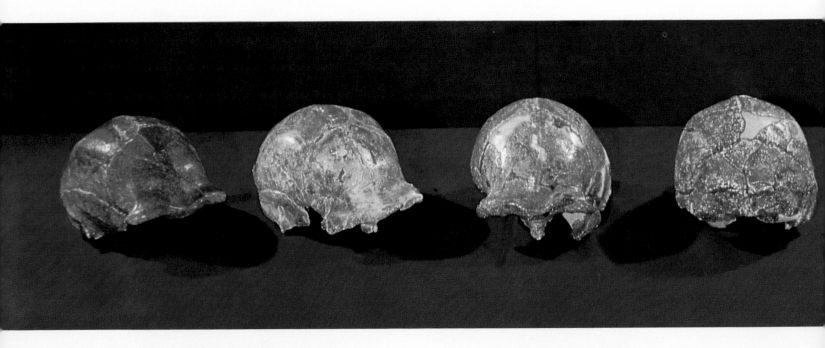

Skull-caps (casts) of Peking Man.

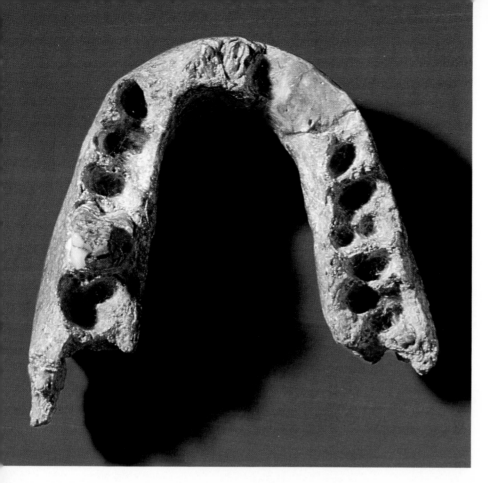

Mandible (lower jaw bone, occlusal view) of Peking Man found after 1949. (68.4 mm)

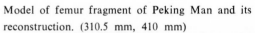

Model of femur fragment of Peking Man and its reconstruction. (310.5 mm, 410 mm)

Skull-cap bones of Peking Man found in 1966. (occipital bone 110.1 mm, frontal bone 121 mm)

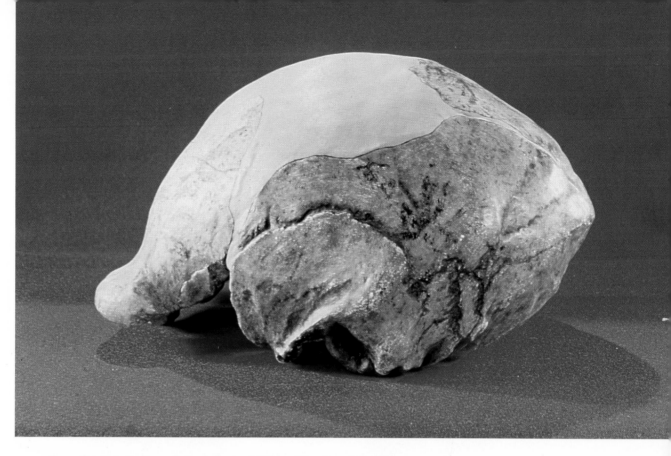

Reconstructed skull-cap (lateral view) of Peking Man found in 1966.

◁Peking Man site.

Reconstructed skull-cap (top view) of Peking Man found in 1966. (207 mm)

Teeth of Peking Man found in 1966 (buccal view). (7.9 mm)

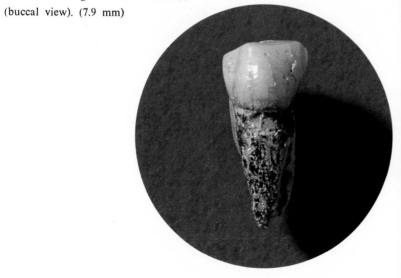

Sculpture: Peking Man making tools.

Discoid chopper of Peking Man. (135 mm)

Stone artifacts of Peking Man. (from Locality 13 of Zhoukoudian). (76 mm, 43 mm, 61 mm)

Scrapers of Peking Man. (88 mm, 100 mm, 70 mm, 35 mm)

Points and burin of Peking Man. (55 mm, 45 mm, 37 mm, 34 mm, 34 mm)

Stone hammers of Peking Man. (117 mm, 146 mm)

Flake and core of Peking Man. (89 mm, 92 mm)

Bipolar flakes of Peking Man. (43 mm, 36 mm, 39 mm, 29 mm)

Chopper and scrapers of Peking Man. (152 mm, 73 mm, 63 mm)

Burned bones and hackberry (*Celtis*) seeds from Peking Man site.

Ash from Peking Man site.

Peking Man used fire.

Antler of *Megaloceros flabellatus* (giant deer) from Locality 13 of Zhoukoudian.

Reconstruction of *Megaloceros flabellatus*.

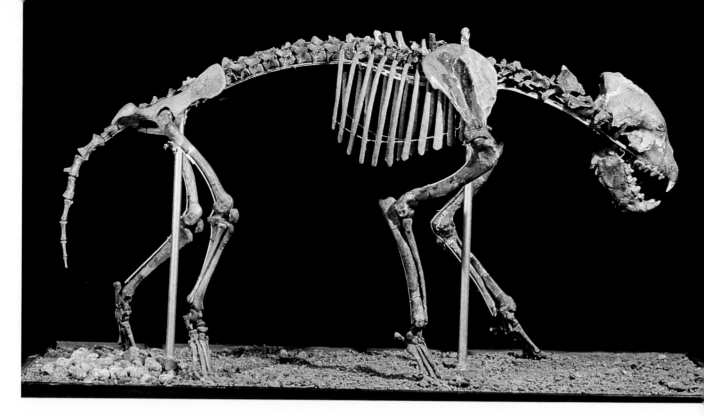

Skeleton of *Hyaena sinensis* from Peking Man site.

Reconstruction of *Hyaena sinensis*.

49

Sabre-toothed cat.

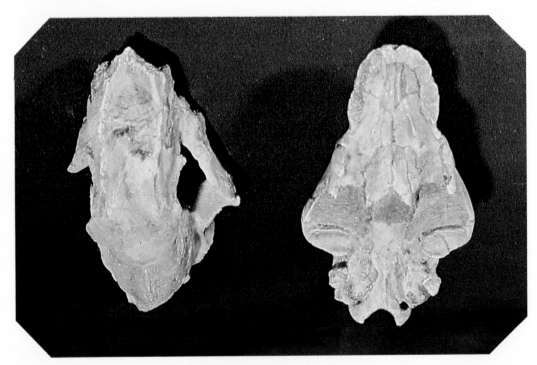

Skull of *Megantereon inexpectatus*
(sabre-toothed cat) from Zhoukoudian.

Skull of *Equus sanmeniensis* (Sanmen horse) from Peking Man site. (occlusal view)

Antler of *Pseudaxis grayi* (deer) from Locality 13 of Zhoukoudian.

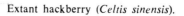
Extant hackberry (*Celtis sinensis*).

Extant peashrub (*Caragana*).

Extant redbud (*Cercis chinensis*).

Ape-man.

北京猿人展览馆

Exhibition Hall of Peking Man site.

Exhibition Hall of Peking Man site (interior).

Jinniushan Hill, Yingkou

In 1974, several fossiliferous sites were found in a cave and some fissures in Jinniushan Hill, Yingkou, Liaoning Province when a quarry was being started. Excavation was undertaken and traces of human activities were found at two sites. Continued excavation in 1975—1976 brought to light a few paleolithic stone artifacts, traces of the use of fire and a wealth of mammalian fossil remains.

The cave was rich in the traces of the use of fire, with a great deal of charred bones, charcoal, and ash. Only a few dozen paleolithic stone artifacts manufactured by hammer flaking or bipolar flaking were found. Most of them were scrapers; there was only one point. They were crudely made, with the exception of two semicircular scrapers somewhat finer in trimming. Judged from the manufacture and form of the stone implements found here, this culture has close affinities with the culture of Peking Man.

The fossil mammalian remains recovered from the lower cultural layer of Jinniushan Hill represented 26 species, such as *Equus sanmeniensis* (horse), *Megaloceros pachyosteus* (giant deer), *Cervus canadensis* (deer) and *Macaca robustus* (monkey), similar to those uncovered at the upper part of the site of Peking Man, suggesting a warm, humid climate.

Scrapers from lower cultural layer of Jinniushan site, Yingkou. (30 mm, 35 mm) (E122°10′, N48°40′)

Paleolithic site of Jinniushan Hill, Yingkou.

Flake from lower cultural layer of Jinniushan site. (58 mm)

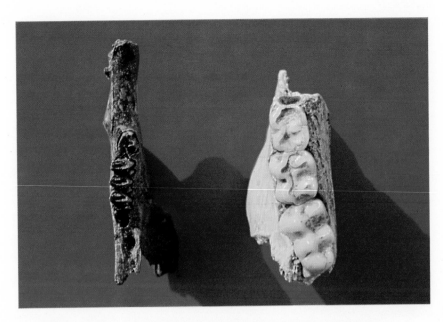

Mandible (lower jaw bone) of *Lepus wongi* (rabbit) and fragment of maxilla (upper jaw bone) of *Macaca robusta* (monkey) from lower cultural layer of Jinniushan site. (occlusal view) (49 mm, 42 mm)

Mandible (lower jaw bone) of *Canis variabilis* (wolf) (buccal view). (149 mm)

PALEOANTHROPIC STAGE

Fossil remains and cultural relics of the Paleoanthropic stage have been found both south and north of the Changjiang (Yangtze) River. Morphologically, the Paleoanthropic man had a less receding forehead, thinner cranial walls and less glabella prominence than the Protoanthropic man. He inherited and developed the Protoanthropic culture in China. Advances were evident in the manufacture of stone tools: with few exceptions, hammer flaking had absolute predominance, with bipolar flaking and stone-on-stone flaking gradually losing ground; the prepared platform technique came into use; the stone flakes became more regular in shape, finer in trimming and more fixed in variety, and also showed a decrease in size.

There were also changes in the composition of mammals. Those of the Tertiary period had disappeared altogether. About 20—30 per cent of all the mammals living in this stage have become extinct. On the other hand, there was a marked increase in the modern species like *Cervus canadensis* (deer), *Megaloceros ordosianus* (deer), *Gazella przewalskyi, Bos primigenius* (bison), *Equus caballus* (horse), *Equus hemionus* (donkey), *Coelodonta antiquitatis* (woolly rhinoceros) and *Mammuthus* (mammoth).

Zhoukoudian, Beijing (Peking)

Locality 15

About 100 meters to the south of the site of Peking Man is a major site which yielded many Paleolithic Age relics—Locality 15 of Zhoukoudian. It was discovered in 1930 and excavated in 1934 and 1935, bringing to light a large number of paleolithic stone artifacts, traces of the use of fire and fossils of 78 species of animals of which 45 were birds and 33 mammals.

The stone implements found show marked advances. The makers knew how to prepare platforms and flaked with a working sequence. The scrapers and points are finely finished and relatively fixed in type. The big stone flakes with shaped handles were effective choppers and were of a special type.

Among the fossil remains of the symbiotic mammals were a few *Megaloceros pachyosteus* (giant deer) fossils. Apart from fossils of *Cervus canadensis* (deer), there were fossil remains of *Gazella Przewalskyi,* a species unknown in the middle Pleistocene, but common in the late Pleistocene. The appearance of this species and the advances manifested in the stone implements show that it is appropriate to place Locality 15 of Zhoukoudian as middle Paleolithic Age.

Locality 15 of Zhoukoudian. (E155°55′, N39°40′)

Burin from Loc. 15 of Zhoukoudian. (52 mm)

Points from Loc. 15 of Zhoukoudian. (52 mm, 29 mm, 48 mm)

Scrapers from Loc. 15 of Zhoukoudian. (48 mm, 47 mm, 39 mm)

Big flake from Loc. 15 of Zhoukoudian. (210 mm)

Chopper from Loc. 15 of Zhoukoudian. (148 mm)

Stone hammer from Loc. 15 of Zhoukoudian. (164 mm)

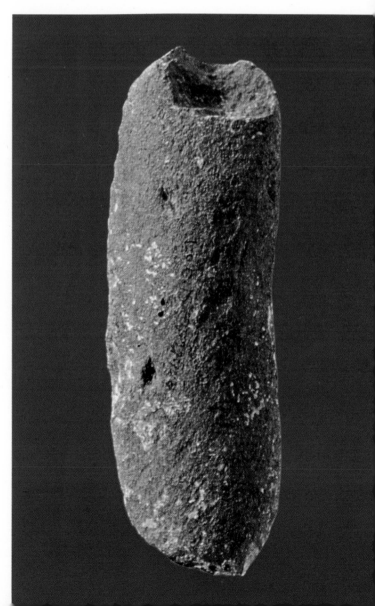

Core from Loc. 15 of Zhoukoudian. (52 mm)

Chopper from Loc. 15 of Zhoukoudian. (84 mm)

Scraper and flake from Loc. 15 of Zhoukoudian.

Horn core of *Gazella przewalskyi* from Loc. 15 of Zhoukoudian. (143 mm)

Maxilla (upper jaw bone) of *Coelodonta antiquitatis* (woolly rhinoceros) from Loc. 15 of Zhoukoudian (occlusal view). (264 mm)

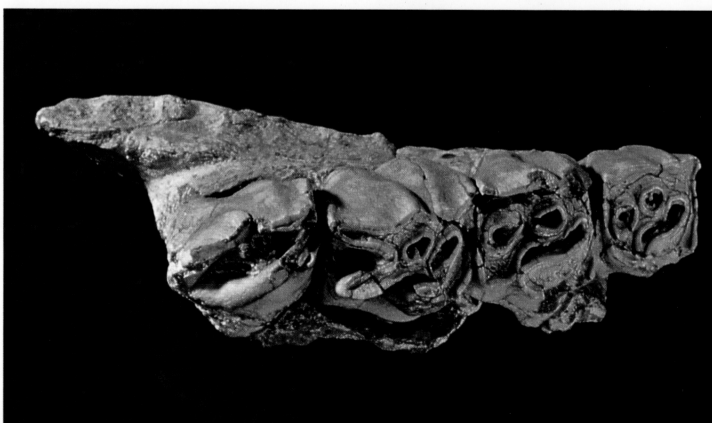

Xindong Man

In 1967, a group of young people visiting the site of Peking Man and Longgushan Hill accidently found a new cave—the Xindong Cave.

Xindong Cave (New Cave) on the south slope of Longgushan Hill is to the north of and linked with the former Locality 4. In 1973 a systematic excavation was carried out, resulting in the discovery of an upper left first premolar of a human being, fossil remains of more than 40 species of mammals, stone artifacts and ash. The mammals included both now extinct *Megaloceros pachyosteus* (giant deer), *Lepus* cf. *wongi* (rabbit), *Equus sanmeniensis* (horse), *Coelodonta* (woolly rhinoceros) and living species such as *Sciurotamias davidianus* (squirrel) and *Cervus canadensis* (deer). Xindong (New-Cave) Man lived in the late Pleistocene epoch, about halfway between Peking Man and Upper Cave Man.

Only a few stone artifacts were recovered, of which one or two were of fine workmanship, resembling stone artifacts found at Locality 15 of Zhoukoudian.

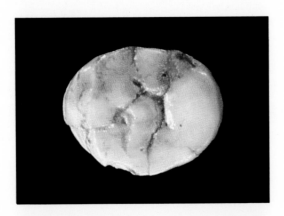

Premolar of New-Cave Man (occlusal view).
(11 mm) (E155°55′, N39°40′)

Premolar of New-Cave Man (lateral view).

The New-Cave site.

Point of New-Cave Man. (59 mm)

Scrapers of New-Cave Man. (39 mm, 38 mm, 58 mm)

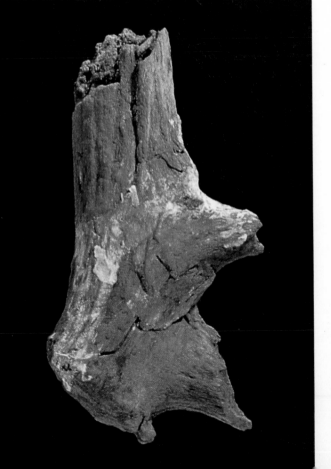

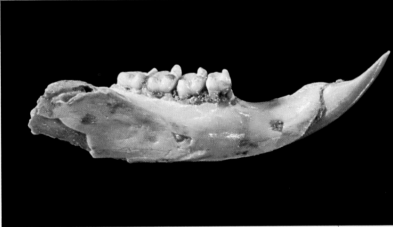

Mandible (lower jaw bone) of *Sciurotamias davi-dianus* (squirrel) from New-Cave of Zhoukoudian (lateral view). (29.9 mm)

Antler of *Cervus elaphus* (deer) from New-Cave. (173 mm)

A new site yielding fossils and stone artifacts was found and excavated in 1957 on the east bank of the Zhoukou Stream and was named Locality 22 of Zhoukoudian. The site is in a fissure on the southwest side of Taipingshan Hill, about 40 meters above water level. Fossils of 10 species of mammals, and 5 quartz implements were recovered from a red clayey deposit. This site may be of the same period as Locality 15 of Zhoukoudian, or slightly later.

Scrapers from Loc. 22 of Zhoukoudian.
(68 mm, 42 mm, 48 mm) (E115°55′, N39°40′)

Dingcun (Tingtsun) Man

The sites which yielded Dingcun paleolithic cultural relics are in the vicinity of Dingcun Village (south from Chaizhuang Village to Shicun Village in the north) in Xiangfen County, Shanxi Province. The sites were discovered in 1953 and extensive investigations were conducted in September 1954, concentrating on twelve sites, out of which ten produced paleolithic stone artifacts. Fossils of three human teeth were found in the sandy gravel at Locality 54:100. Further excavation of this site in September 1976 yielded the fossil of an infant's right parietal. As all the fossils were found near Dingcun Village, the find was designated "Dingcun Man".

The three teeth—an upper right median incisor, an upper right second incisor and a lower right second molar—belonged to a child of about 12 years old. The right parietal was that of an infant of two or three years old. These fossils indicate that morphologically Dingcun Man was about halfway between ape-man and modern man, and closely related to Hetao Man (Ordos Man). The incisors of Dingcun Man were shovel-shaped, similar to those of the modern Mongoloid, but different from those of the Europoid.

More than 2,000 paleolithic stone artifacts have been unearthed at these sites. The stone flakes and implements were large and crude. Stone-on-stone flaking played an important role in flaking, so the stone flakes were thick and broad, with sloping platforms and large angles, usually over 120°. Among the stone tools, there were many more choppers than scrapers and points. They also included a few stone balls. The large prismatic point was of a unique variety. Due to these salient features of the stone implements they were given the name of "Dingcun Culture".

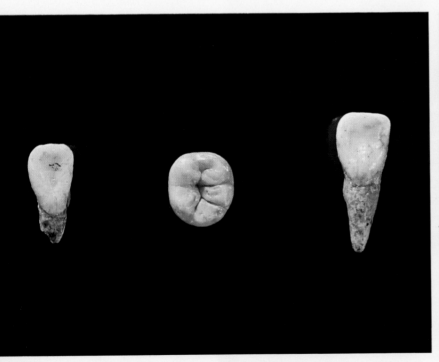

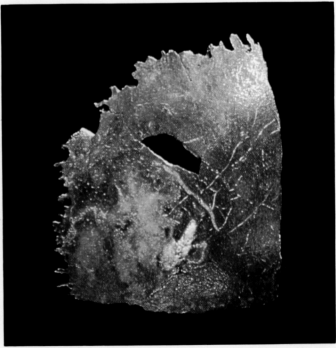

Teeth of Dingcun (Tingtsun) Man. (lat. incisor 10.1 mm, molar 10.1 mm, med. incisor 8.3 mm) (E111°30′, N35°50′)

Parietal bone (vertex bone of skull) of Dingcun Man. (55 mm)

Site of Dingcun Man.

Big point of Dingcun Man. (185 mm)

Points of Dingcun Man. (82 mm, 64 mm, 46 mm)

Site of Dingcun Man.

Chopper of Dingcun Man. (195 mm)

Discoid core of Dingcun Man. (121 mm)

Chopper of Dingcun Man. (164 mm)

Chopper of Dingcun Man. (160 mm)

Flake and scraper of Dingcun Man. (107 mm, 83 mm)

Stone ball of Dingcun Man. (90 mm)

The woolly rhinoceros.

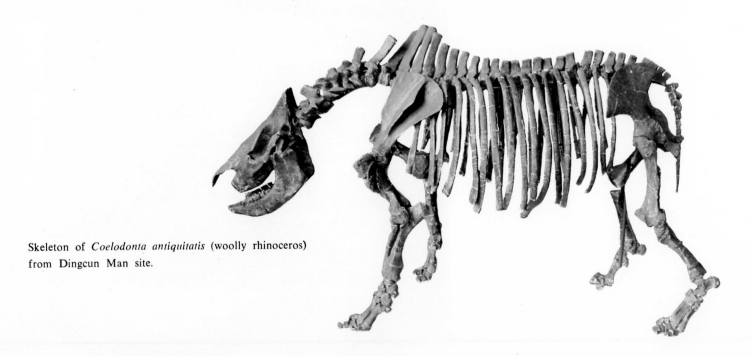

Skeleton of *Coelodonta antiquitatis* (woolly rhinoceros) from Dingcun Man site.

Bos primigenius (primitive bison).

Horn core of *Bos primigenius* from Dingcun Man site.

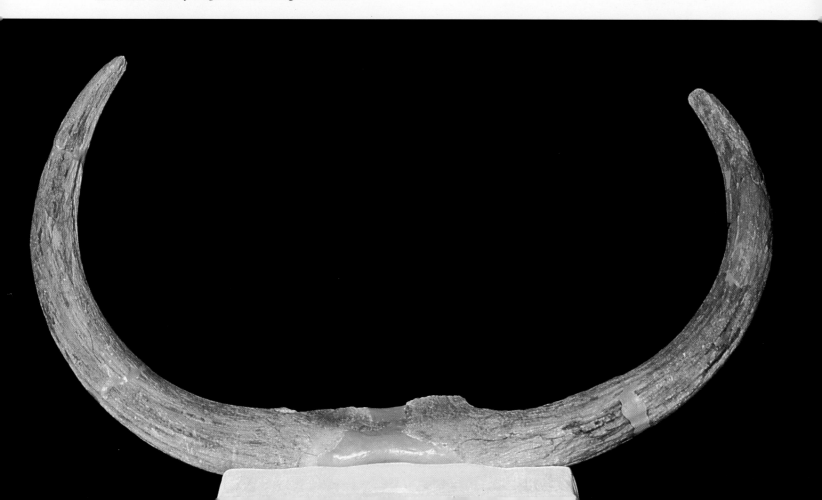

A group of Dingcun Man hunting.

Fanjiazhuang, Jiaocheng

In the summer of 1957, a group of paleoanthropologists on field investigation found a number of paleolithic stone artifacts at Fanjiazhuang Village northwest of Jiaocheng county in Shanxi Province. The stone artifacts were mostly cores and flakes, with stone tools—scrapers, points and choppers—accounting for only 2 per cent. The flakes and stone tools were quite small, with the exception of few crude and heavy ones. Hammering seems to have been the chief method of flaking and trimming. From this the inference is that these paleolithic stone artifacts are slightly younger than Dingcun Culture.

Point and scraper from Jiaocheng, Shanxi Province.
(35 mm, 29 mm) (E112°10′, N37°35′)

Scraper from Jiaocheng. (40 mm)

Chopper from Jiaocheng. (114 mm)

Xigou, Licun Village, Quwo

The site producing the paleolithic stone artifacts at Xigou, Licun Village, Quwo County, Shanxi Province was discovered and trial-excavated in 1956. The site is about 5 kilometers south of the Dingcun sites and 40 meters above the Fenhe River. One hundred and seventy-two paleolithic stone artifacts, mostly flakes and cores, were recovered in the sandy gravel. The stone tools, few and small, include some scrapers and points. They were mainly made of hornfels, the same material used in the Dingcun Culture. While sharing certain features in manufacture, the stone artifacts found here and those at Dingcun show marked differences in form and trimming technique, the former undoubtedly younger than the latter. Inclusion of them in the Dingcun Culture, therefore, would complicated the study of the development of Dingcun Culture.

Point and scrapers from Licunxigou in Quwo County, Shanxi Province. (17 mm, 26 mm, 23 mm) (E111°35′, N35°45′)

Scrapers from Licunxigou in Quwo County. (81 mm, 52 mm)

Gezidong Cave, Kazou

Gezidong Cave in the Kazou Monggol (Mongolian) Autonomous County, Liaoning Province, yielded paleolithic cultural relics. It is a cave-fissure site situated close to the Dalinghe River and 35 meters above water level. The two excavations in 1973 and 1975 unearthed, in the breccia and the layer of ash, some 300 paleolithic stone artifacts, traces of the use of fire and fossil remains of 31 species of mammals including *Crocuta ultima* (hyena), *Cervus canadensis* (deer) and *Gazella przewalskyi*. Of these species, 25.8 per cent are now extinct. Fossils of the fauna in Gezidong Cave, for example fossils of *Pseudois* cf. *nayaur* (goat), indicate that the climate at that time was colder than that of today. The abundance of fossil remains of desert-prairie animals shows that the climate was also slightly drier.

The paleolithic stone artifacts recovered in Gezidong Cave are, for the most part, small in size, the majority being scrapers and the rest points and choppers. In flaking, type, manufacturing technique and size, they bear resemblance to, but also show certain improvements over those of Peking Man and those discovered at Locality 15 of Zhoukoudian. They are therefore believed to have been the continuation and development of the last two. In the light of the analysis of both the stone implements and animal fossils, it may be assumed that this site belonged to the middle Paleolithic Age, possibly later than Locality 15 of Zhoukoudian.

Flakes from Gezidong (Pigeon Cave) of Kazuo County, Liaoning Province. (58 mm, 46 mm) (E119°50′, N41°15′)

Chopper from Gezidong Cave of Kazuo County. (156 mm)

Gezidong Cave.

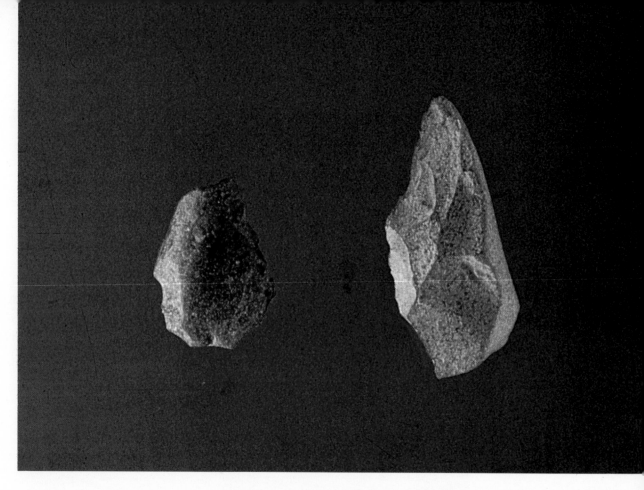

Points from Gezidong site of Kazuo. (44 mm, 71 mm)

Scrapers from Gezidong site. (57 mm, 61 mm)

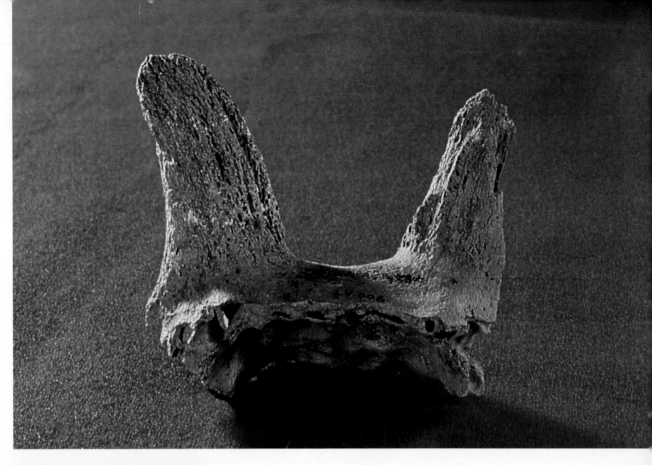

Horn core of *Pseudois* cf. *nayaur* (blue sheep) from Gezidong site. (77 mm)

Horn core of *Gazella przewalskyi* from Gezidong site. (165 mm)

Maba (Mapa) Man

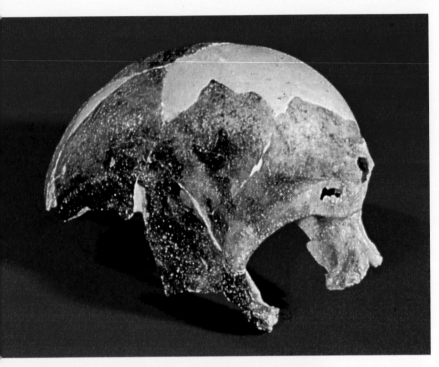

The fossils of Maba Man were found in June 1958, in a cave in Shizifeng Hill, Maba Township, Qujiang County, Guangdong Province.

Of the three layers of karst caves in Shizifeng Hill, human fossil and most of the animal fossil remains were unearthed in the second layer of the deposit in the cave. The animal fossils represented *Hyaena*, *Ursus* (bear), *Ailuropoda* (giant panda), *Panthera* cf. *tigris* (tiger), *Tapirus*, *Rhinoceros sinensis*, *Cervus Rhizomy* (bamboo rat), *Stegodon* (elephant), *Paleoloxodon namadicus* (elephant), and others. Their geologic age is probably the early part of the late Pleistocene.

The Maba Man fossil is an incomplete skull of a middle-aged male composing of a frontal bone, part of a parietal bone, the right eye orbit and a good part of a nasal bone. Maba Man is comparable to Solo Man of Java.

Fossil skull of Maba (Mapa) Man. (E113°30′, N24°45′) (lateral view)

Fossil skull of Maba Man. (140 mm) (top view)

A distant view of Maba Man site.

Maba Man site.

Reconstruction of Maba Man.

Changyang Man

Fossil remains of Changyang Man were found by local inhabitants at Xiazhongjiawan, Zhaojia-yan District, Changyang County, Hubei Province. A study group from the Laboratory of Vertebrate Paleontology did field research and investigations as well as excavations in 1957.

The fossil remains were represented by a fragmentary left maxilla carrying a first premolar and a first molar, and a lower left second premolar. Changyang Man retained certain primitive features, but showed more features of modern man.

In the stratum which yielded Changyang Man fossil remains were also found fossils of animals such as *Hystrix* (porcupine), *Rhizomys* (bamboo rat), *Cuon antiquus* (jackal), *Cuon* sp., *Ursus augustus* (bear), *Ailuropoda melanoleuca* (giant panda), *Felidae indet* (cat), *Meles* sp. (badger), *Hyaena sinensis, Stegodon orientalis* (elephant), *Megatapirus* and *Rhinoceros sinensis*. Their geologic age is the beginning of the late Pleistocene.

A distant view of Changyang Man site. (E110°35′, N30°15′)

Changyang Man site.

Maxilla (upper jaw bone) (basal view)
of Changyang Man. (44.5 mm)

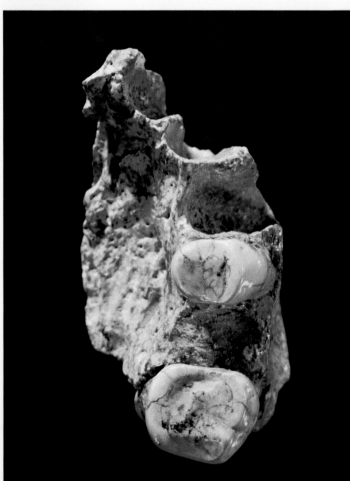

Premolar (occlusal view) of Changyang Man. (10.6 mm)

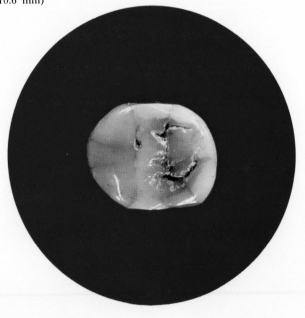

90

Teeth (occlusal view) of *Hystrix* cf. *subcristata* (porcupine) from Changyang
Man site. (9.3 mm, 8.2 mm)

Maxilla (upper jaw bone) of Bovidae (bison) (basal view) from Changyang
Man site. (51.5 mm)

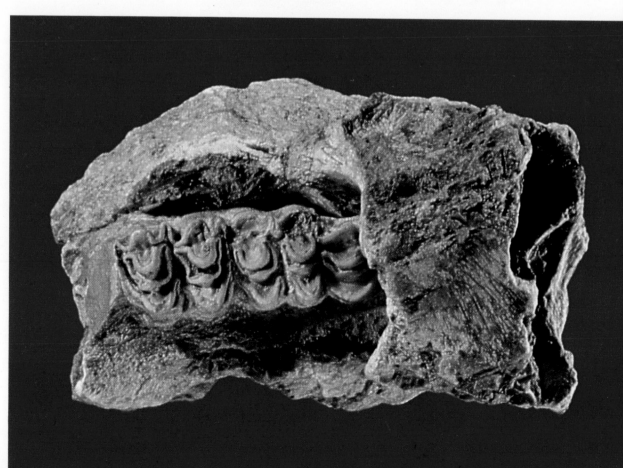

Tongzi Man

Tongzi Man was discovered in a limestone cave about 15 kilometers northwest of the Tongzi County seat in Guizhou Province. The fossil remains of Tongzi Man are two teeth—an upper right median incisor belonging to an aged individual and an upper right first premolar belonging to a young individual. The two teeth are somewhat different in shape from those of modern man, and rather resemble those of Peking Man. The fossil remains of Tongzi Man, though few in number, are of considerable value because they are the human fossils ever found on the Yunnan-Guizhou Plateau.

Along with these fossil teeth were found stone implements and fossil remains of mammals, among which *Hystrix magna* (porcupine), *Cuon javanicus, Ailuropoda* (giant panda), *Crocuta ultima* (hyena), *Stegodon orientalis* (elephant), *Magatapirus* and *Rhinoceros sinensis* have been identified as members of what is commonly known as *Ailuropoda-Stegodon* fauna in South China. The geologic age represented by this fauna is middle and late Pleistocene.

The 12 stone artifacts excavated in this limestone cave bear comparison with those found in Guanyindong Cave at Qianxi, exhibiting possible cultural ties. But the former is of a later period.

Tongzi Man site. (E106°45′, N28°15′)

A distant view of Tongzi Man site.

Teeth of Tongzi Man. (7.2 mm, 9.1 mm)

Chopper of Tongzi Man. (121 mm)

Scraper of Tongzi Man. (83 mm)

Molar (occlusal view) of *Hylobates* sp.
(gibbon) from Tongzi Man site.
(7 mm)

Extant gibbon.

Extant golden monkey.

Teeth of *Rhinopithecus* sp. (golden
monkey) from Tongzi Man site.
(occlusal view) (8.3 mm, 8.0 mm, 11.0
mm, 11.3 mm)

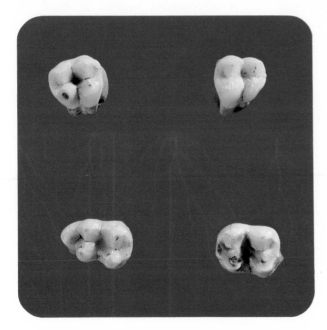

Jiangjiawan, Zhenyuan

In 1965, forty paleolithic stone artifacts and some mammalian fossils were found in the late Pleistocene stratum at Jiangjiawan (on the west bank of the Bajiazui Reservoir) in Zhenyuan County, Gansu Province. Most of the stone artifacts are choppers and scrapers and some are stone balls, all crudely made with stone hammers. The paleolithic stone implements of this site are similar in type and manufacture to their contemporaries in North China, indicating close cultural ties between them. According to available data, the culture of this site has been estimated to belong to middle Paleolithic period. The discovery of this site bridges the gap between Lantian Man and Shuidonggou Culture in Northwest China.

Scrapers and point from Jiangjiawan site, Zhenyuan County, Gansu Province. (81 mm, 43 mm, 52 mm) (E107°20′, N35°35′)

Shuicheng Man

Shuicheng Man was found in a Xiaohui cave on the right bank of the Sanchahe River, 25 kilometers northwest of the Shuicheng County seat in Guizhou Province. The site was discovered in the summer of 1973 and excavated in the winter of the same year and the following spring. A human tooth fossil, a layer of ash, stone artifacts and a few fossils of mammals including *Stegodon* were found in the cave.

Shuicheng Man is represented by a large upper right canine belonging to a male. Morphologically, Shuicheng Man is more developed than Peking Man but more primitive than Liujiang Man and Upper Cave Man. Although not many stone implements were recovered in this cave, they could represent a new regional culture because they were manufactured mainly by bipolar flaking of a special type (in which the striking force acted more or less slopingly instead of acting vertically). In view of these facts, Shuicheng Man has tentatively been placed as belonging to late Pleistocene. However, data on hand are insufficient to determine whether Shuicheng Man should fall into the category of the Paleoanthropic or the Neoanthropic stage. For convenience of treatment, Shuicheng Man is put as at the end of the Paleoanthropic Stage.

Canine of Shuicheng Man. (9.3 mm)
(E104°50′, N26°50′) (occlusal view)

Canine of Shuicheng Man.
(buccal view)

Scrapers of Suicheng Man. (56 mm, 84 mm)

Flake of Shuicheng Man. (81 mm)

97

Rejiuqu, Dingri

In 1964, a scientific investigation team of Xizang (Tibet) discovered 40 paleolithic stone artifacts on the 20-m. terrace at Rejiuqu, 10 kilometers southeast of the Dingri County seat during its field work in the Xixiabangma area. All the stone artifacts are either flakes or flake tools made with stone hammers. They are similar to the paleolithic stone artifacts found further to the east both in tool assemblage and in the dominance of trimming from the main flaking surface to the back. Analysis of the type and trimming technique of these stone implements dates them to the middle or late Paleolithic Age. However, in the absence of stratigraphic and paleontological data, more exact dating is extremely difficult. The fossil site of Rejiuqu is arranged at the end of the Paleoanthropic stage, as in the case of Suicheng Man.

Point and scrapers from Rejiuqu, Dingri. (49 mm, 58 mm, 70 mm) (E87°21′, N28°45′)

NEOANTHROPIC STAGE

Primitive man's entry into the Neoanthropic stage about 40,000 years ago was accompanied by marked bodily and cultural changes. Morphologically, he was not much different from modern man. Compared with the Paleoanthropic man, he had a more vaulted skull with the broadest part near the parietal tubercle, shorter and lower superciliary arches and a better-developed forehead. The occipital bone was higher. The position of occipital orifice (*Foramen magnum*) is close to the center of the skull bottom. The facial skeleton was relatively shorter and with less prognathism, the cranial capacity was ranging from 1,300—1,500 c.c. and the teeth smaller. Liujiang Man, Ziyang Man and Upper Cave Man found in China all bore skull features of the primitive Mongoloid and were representatives of the early Mongoloid. The Neoanthropic stage witnessed faster and marked cultural development. The stone implements became more fixed in type and smaller in size. Indirect flaking technique and trimming by pressure were possibly in use. The polished bone artifacts and the abundance of perforated ornaments found in a number of sites evidence human mastery of polishing and drilling techniques at that time. The presence of eyed needles of bone shows that man had already learnt to make clothes. The discovery of graves points to the development of human consciousness. All these facts indicate that culturally the Neoanthropic stage was far ahead of any previous stage and paved the way for faster development to a more advanced stage of primitive society—the Neolithic Age.

The natural environment also underwent noticeable changes in this stage. The extinct species of mammals became less and less, accounting for less than 10 per cent of all the mammals, and in their place came large numbers of mammalian species still extant today. The representative faunal fossils of this stage were those of *Coelodonta* (woolly rhinoceros), *Mammuthus* (mammoth), *Megaloceros ordosianus* (deer), *Cervus canadensis* (deer), *Gazella przewalskyi, Equus caballus* (horse) and *Equus hemionus* (donkey).

Jianping Man

The Jianping Man fossil was discovered in 1957 in a purchasing center at Chengguan Townlet in Jianping County, Liaoning Province. It was a highly fossilized right upper arm bone. It is said that along with Jianping Man in the same stratum, there might have been fossil remains of *Coelodonta antiquitatis* (woolly rhinoceros), *Spirocerus* cf. *kiakhtensis* (antelope), *Bison priscus, Equus hemionus* (donkey) and *Equus* cf. *przewalskyi* (horse). The fossil probably belongs to the late Pleistocene.

The upper arm bone of Jianping Man was the first human fossil found in Liaoning Province. It is a tentative clue to the distribution of the primitive man in the late Pleistocene epoch.

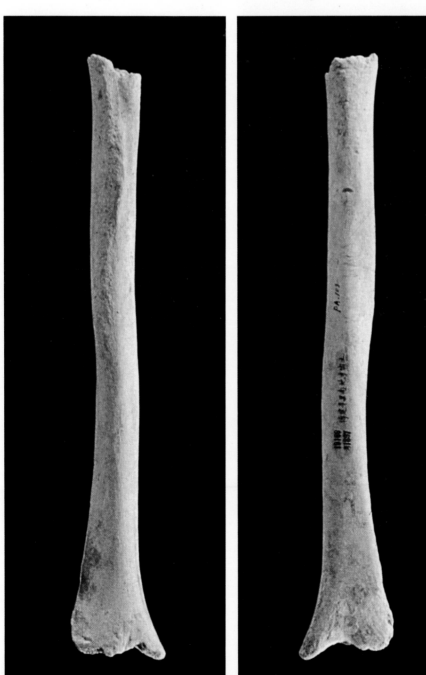

Humerus (upper arm bone) of Jianping Man.
(256 mm) (E119°30′, N41°20′)
(anterior view)

Humerus of Jianping Man.
(posterior view)

Xibajianfang, Lingyuan

Stone tools from Xibajianfang, Lingyuan County, Liaoning Province. (39 mm, 31 mm, 36 mm, 41 mm) (E119°30′, N41°19′)

The site yielding cultural relics of the late Paleolithic Age at Xibajianfang in Lingyuan County, Liaoning Province, was discovered in 1972. The two excavations in 1972 and 1973 unearthed 49 paleolithic stone artifacts, scattered traces of the use of fire and a few fossil remains of mammals such as *Bos primigenius* (bison). The stone implements, chiefly scrapers and points, were small in size, mostly trimmed from the main surface to the back. These paleolithic stone implements, though few in number, present general features of the late Paleolithic Age in China, and are considered reliable evidence of the existence of a paleolithic culture in Northeast China, and therefore will lead to further investigations.

Paleolithic site at Xibajianfang.

Jinniushan Hill, Yingkou

The upper cultural layers of Jinniushan Hill near Yingkou are those above the third layer in a cave-fissure deposit on the west side of the hill. Uncovered in this series of layers were fossil remains of 21 species of mammals such as *Coelodonta antiquitatis* (woolly rhinoceros). The fauna of this site are similar to that of the Upper Cave. Excavations of the first layer (excluding the surface soil) in 1974 unearthed an eyed bone implement made of a deer's (?) coccygeal vertebra cut in half. In 1975, a polished bone awl was found in the second layer. Polished bone implements are considered one of the important cultural achievements of the late Paleolithic Age. The characteristics of the polished bone implements and the fauna are consistent with the conclusion that the upper cultural layers of Jinniushan Hill belong to the late Paleolithic Age.

Bone tools from upper cultural layer of Jinniushan site, Yingkou. (69 mm, 66 mm) (E122°30′, N40°40′)

Shibazhan, Huma

The site of the Paleolithic Age cultural relics at Shibazhan in Huma County, Heilungjiang Province, was discovered in 1975 and excavated in 1976. In the boulder clay on the second terrace (about 15 meters above the local water level) by the Huma River several hundred stone artifacts were found, mostly stone flakes bearing distinct traditional features of microlithic technique. Analysis of the geomorphological and other data suggests that this site dates back to the late Paleolithic Age.

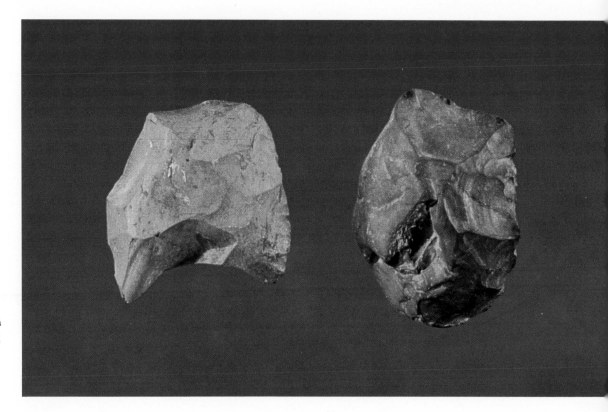

Stone tools from Shibazhan, Huma County, Heilongjiang Province. (81 mm, 97 mm) (E125°35′, N52°25′)

Zhaocun Village, Qian'an

The paleolithic site at Zhaocun Village in Qian'an County, Hebei Province, was found and excavated in 1958 and re-examined in 1973. Altogether 22 paleolithic stone artifacts and fossil remains of seven species of mammals were unearthed, including an elephant's tusk which was examined by Comrade Mao Tsetung in 1958 during his inspection of the achievements in scientific research by the Chinese Academy of Sciences. Among the paleolithic stone artifacts are bipolar flakes, scrapers, points and choppers. According to the data available, this site could be of the late Paleolithic Age.

Tusk of *Elephas* cf. *namadicus* (elephant) from Zhaocun, Qian'an, Hebei Province. (E118°40', N39°55')

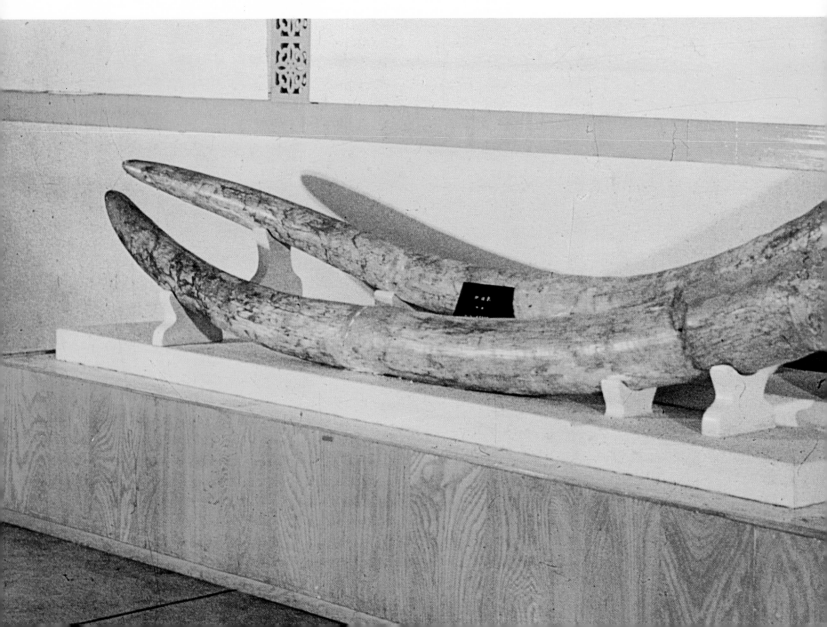

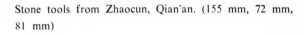

Stone tools from Zhaocun, Qian'an. (155 mm, 72 mm, 81 mm)

Hutouliang, Yangyuan

In 1972, a cluster of Stone Age sites was found at Hutouliang in Yangyuan County, Hebei Province. Nine sites were discovered within less than 10 kilometers, each yielding an abundance of stone artifacts. The stone implements excavated at Hutouliang, especially the points and scrapers, are noted for their fine trimming. Among them, there are wedge-cores in the tradition of microlithic technique and two stone implements showing traces of polishing over portions of their surfaces. The stone implements of Hutouliang display a marked technological refinement. Their geologic age could be the end of the late Old Stone Age.

Paleolithic site at Hutuoliang, Yangyuan County, Hebei Province. (E114°30′, N40°15′)

Points from Hutuoliang site.
(57 mm, 55 mm, 49 mm)

End scrapers from Hutuoliang site.
(40 mm, 32 mm)

Upper Cave Man

Upper Cave Man, as its name implies, was found in a cave on the upper part of the hill where the Peking Man site is situated. Excavations were undertaken in 1933 and the following spring.

The fossil remains of Upper Cave Man include three complete skulls, fragments of body bones and individual teeth. All of these fossils presumably belonged to ten, or at least eight, individuals: an aged male, a male between thirty and fifty, two middle-aged females, a young individual, a teenager, a five-year-old child and an infant or fetus. Of the morphological features of the Upper Cave Man skull, some are primitive features common to Neoanthropic fossils, some are similar to those of the present-day Mongoloid, especially the Chinese, the Eskimos and the North American Indians, and some with features different from the typical present-day Mongoloid but identical with those of other Neoanthropic fossils discovered in China.

Few stone implements together with some bone artifacts were found in the Upper Cave. The Upper Cave Man knew how to make and use polished bone implements such as bone needles. In addition, the 141 articles of personal adornment discovered in this cave show that Upper Cave Man had aesthetic concepts. He also scattered powered hematite (red ochre) around the dead, an expression of primitive religious concepts. He had ideas such as the existence of a soul.

Except for *Crocuta ultima* (hyena) and *Ursus spelaeus* (cave bear), the Upper Cave fauna consist of all living species. The Upper Cave Man site is dated as the final stage of the Pleistocene epoch. Carbon-14 dating places the site about 18,500 years ago.

Fossil skulls (casts) of Upper Cave Man. (129 mm, 123 mm, 135 mm)
(E115°55′, N39°40′)

The Upper Cave (a distant view).

111

The Upper Cave.

Points and scraper of Upper Cave Man.
(62 mm, 37 mm)

Reconstruction of Upper Cave Man.

Scraper of Upper Cave Man. (69 mm)

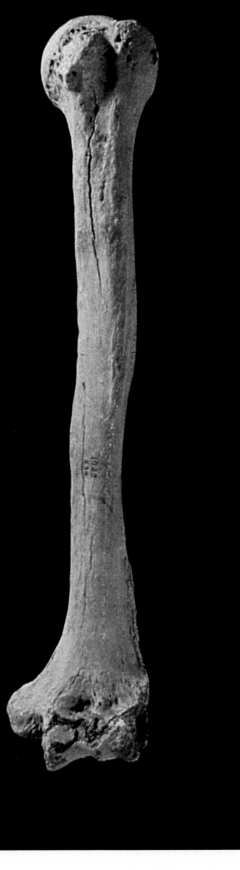

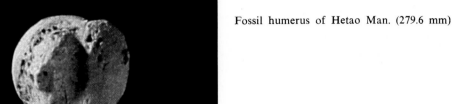
Fossil humerus of Hetao Man. (279.6 mm)

Scrapers of Hetao Man. (26 mm, 28 mm, 27 mm)

Lamawan, Qingshuihe

Stone tools from Lamawan, Qingshuihe, Inner Mongolia. (83 mm, 91 mm) (E110°35′, N40°03′)

In 1958 and 1959 in conjunction with the execution of the Huanghe River (Yellow River) Water Conservancy Project, an investigation of paleolithic stone artifacts was conducted along the Huanghe River, from Togtoh County of the Nei Monggol (Inner Mongolian) Autonomous Region in the north to Pianguan County, Shanxi Province in the south, with Lamawan in Qingshuihe County as the center. Some paleolithic sites were discovered. Only a few crude stone artifacts were actually found in the sandy gravel at the terrace with "pedestal". But a large number of stone artifacts were found on the ground. These stone artifacts, especially points and scrapers, were finely trimmed, comparable with those of Shuidonggou or Hutouliang. As no fossils were found along with the stone artifacts either in the sandy gravel or on the ground, there is difficulty in dating. As regards the form and type, the stone artifacts show some advances over the points found at Shuidonggou, but are slightly inferior to those of Hutouliang. It is inferred that the stone artifacts found on the earth surface may be of late Paleolithic Age and those from the sandy gravel of an earlier date.

Point and scraper from Lamawan, Qingshuihe. (91 mm, 83 mm)

Shuidonggou, Lingwu

Shuidonggou in Lingwu County in the Ningxia Hui Autonomous Region was the first site in China to have yielded paleolithic cultural relics. A research report published in 1928 claimed that the stone artifacts first recovered in 1923 came from one and the same layer. In 1960, several Soviet researchers investigated this site for a period of time, but failed to establish the stratigraphic sequence. This was cleared up by Chinese paleoanthropologists on another excavation there in the summer of 1963. The strata comprise several culture layers. The polished stone axes from the sandy gravel should be dated Neolithic Age whereas the stone artifacts from the sandy soil below represent Shuidonggou Culture of the late Paleolithic Age.

Shuidonggou Culture has its distinctive features. The stone cores are rectangular, semi-conical or cylindrical. Some 40 per cent of the stone artifacts are rectangular flakes which account for 20 per cent of all the flakes. The main types of the stone artifacts are scrapers and points. A few choppers and burins as well as a pierced circular ornament made from a *Struthio* (ostrich) eggshell were also found. In a similar layer nearby were a bone awl and a fairly complete fossil skull of *Bos primigenius* (bison). Judging by the characteristics of the finds at this site, Shuidonggou Culture is assumed to belong to the late Paleolithic Age.

A distant view of Shuidonggou paleolithic site. (E106°40′, N38°10′)

Shuidonggou site.

Points from Shuidonggou site. (52 mm, 56 mm, 60 mm)

End scrapers from Shuidonggou site.
(81 mm, 64 mm, 39 mm)

Scrapers from Shuidonggou site.
(45 mm, 46 mm, 65 mm)

Stone core from Shuidonggou site. (105 mm)

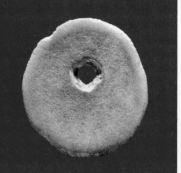

Ornament from Shuidonggou site. (19 mm)

Blades from Shuidonggou site. (65 mm, 68 mm)

Bone awl from Shuidonggou site. (59 mm)

Skull of *Bos primigenius* (bison) from Shuidonggou site.

Loufangzi, Huan Xian

A site yielding paleolithic stone artifacts was found in 1963 at Loufangzi in Huan Xian County, Gansu Province. It is by the Hedaochuan River on the upper reaches of the Malianhe River (Huanjiang River). It was investigated in 1974. In deposit on the second terrace, a large number of mammalian fossils, paleolithic stone artifacts and traces of the use of fire were discovered. The stone artifacts were all small in size, mostly trimmed from the main flaking surface to the back, but they were of fine workmanship and fixed in type. The points and scrapers among them were rather regular. The mammalian fauna, similar to those discovered at Salawusu, included *Coelodonta* (woolly rhinoceros), *Crocuta ultima* and *Megaloceros ordosianus* (deer). Comparison between the paleolithic stone artifacts discovered here and those found elsewhere dates the former as of the late Paleolithic Age.

Points from Loufanzi, Huan Xian, Gansu Province. (48 mm, 47 mm) (E107°40′, N36°20′)

Huohuoxili, Qinghai

A geological field survey carried out in 1956 on the Qinghai Plateau produced five pebble choppers on the bank of the Qushuihe River near Huohuoxili in Qinghai Province where the Changjiang (Yangtze) River rises. These were crudely fashioned and bore distinct Old Stone Age style.

Stone tools from Huohuoxili, Qinghai Province. (103 mm) (E93°15′, N35°25′)

Xiaonanhai, Anyang

Cultural relics of the late Paleolithic Age was found in 1960 in a cave at Xiaonanhai, about 30 kilometers southwest of the city of Anyang, Henan Province. Explorative excavations brought to light more than 7,000 paleolithic stone artifacts, abundant traces of the use of fire and fossils of 17 species of mammals, including *Coelodonta*. Flakes and cores comprise more than 98 per cent of the paleolithic stone artifacts unearthed here, most of them made by bipolar flaking. In abundance of stone implements by bipolar flaking, this site is second only to the site of Peking Man. The similar bipolar flaking technique as used by Peking Man is a distinguishing feature of the Xiaonanhai culture. Unearthed from the deposit in the Xiaonanhai cave were about 100 stone implements, small in size and crude in workmanship, consisting only of scrapers and points. From the composition of the finds the Xiaonanhai cave was likely to have been where stone tools were made.

Stone tools from Xiaonanhai site, Anyang, Henan Province. (35 mm, 32 mm, 44 mm, 16 mm) (E114°05′, N36°0′)

Bipolar flake from Xiaonanhai site. (34 mm)

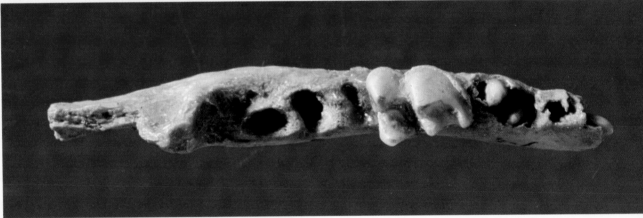

Mandible (lower jaw bone) of *Erinaceus* (hedgehog) (occlusal view) from Xiaonanhai site. (35 mm)

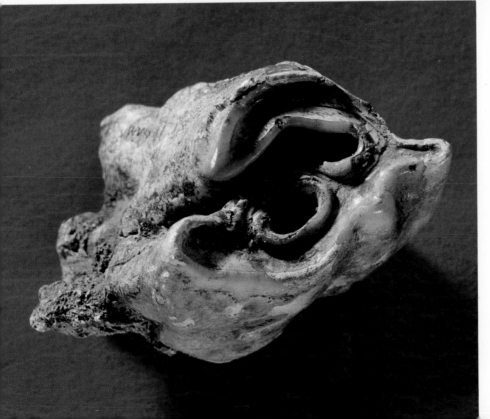

Molar of *Coelodonta antiquitatis* (woolly rhinoceros) (occlusal view) from Xiaonanhai site. (57 mm)

Liujiang (Liuchiang) Man

Liujiang Man fossil remains were found in a small grotto close to Tongtianyan, in Liujiang County, Guangxi Zhuang Autonomous Region. They consisted of a complete skull, four thoracic vertebrae with four ribs of different lengths attached to them, a complete set of lumbar vertebrae, a sacrum, a right hip bone, a fragment of the right femur and a fragment of the left femur. All these belonged to a middle-aged male. It is rare in China for so many parts of the same individual to have been found simultaneously. In the Liujiang Man cave were also fossils of such mammals as *Rhinoceros sinensis, Stegodon* (elephant) and *Megatapirus,* indicating the geologic age to be the late Pleistocene.

From morphological features of the skull, Liujiang Man was ascertained to be of an early type of the Neoanthropic man, more primitive than Zhoukoudian (Choukoutien) Upper Cave Man and Ziyang Man. Liujiang Man was an early type of the Mongoloid race then taking shape, and the earliest Neoanthropic man ever found in China.

A distant view of Liujiang (Liuchiang) Man Cave. (E109°25′, N24°15′)

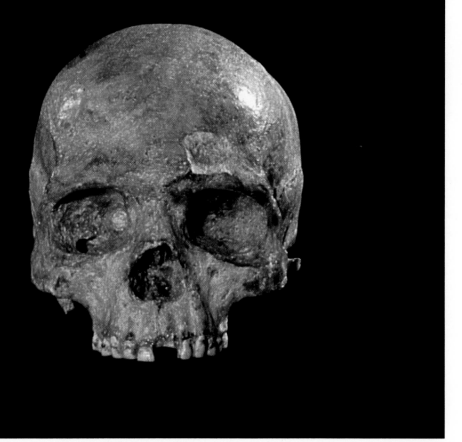

Fossil skull of Liujiang Man (front view) (142.2 mm)

Skull of Liujiang Man (anterio-lateral view).

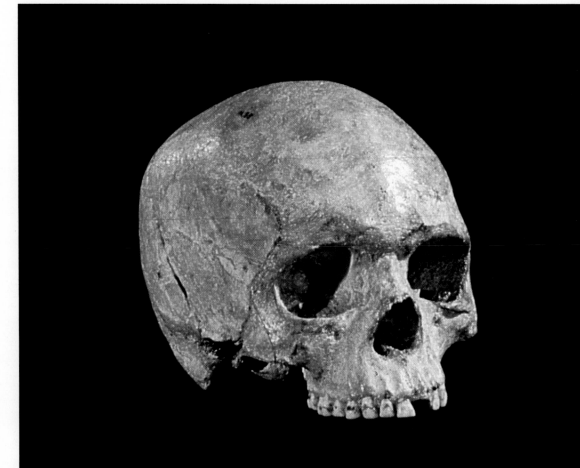

140

Femur (thigh bone) of Liujiang Man. (215 mm, 120 mm)

Bones of Liujiang Man. (187 mm, 200 mm, 144 mm)

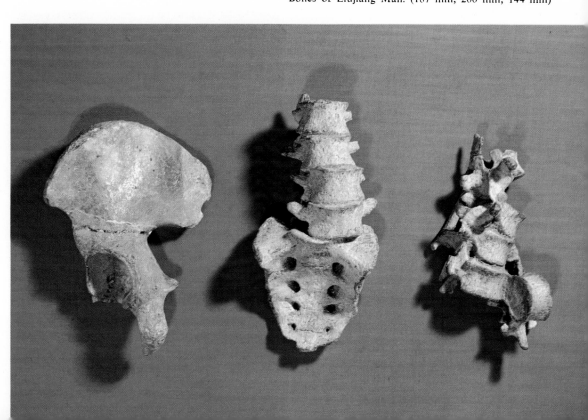

Extant giant panda.

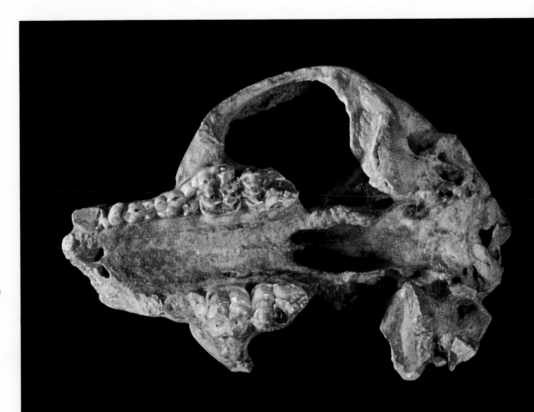

Skull of *Ailuropoda melanoleuca* (giant panda)
from Liujiang Man Cave. (basal view)

142

Qilinshan Man

On January 14, 1956, in a cave in Qilinshan Hill in Laibin County, Guangxi Zhuang Autonomous Region, a fragmentary human skull was discovered and named "Qilinshan Man". Judged by the morphological features, Qilinshan Man was of a Neoanthropic type. Also found in the cave were one stone artifact and two stone flakes. Only a few mammalian fossils were found in the cave: teeth of deer and pig and animal limb fragments. Their geologic age might be late Pleistocene.

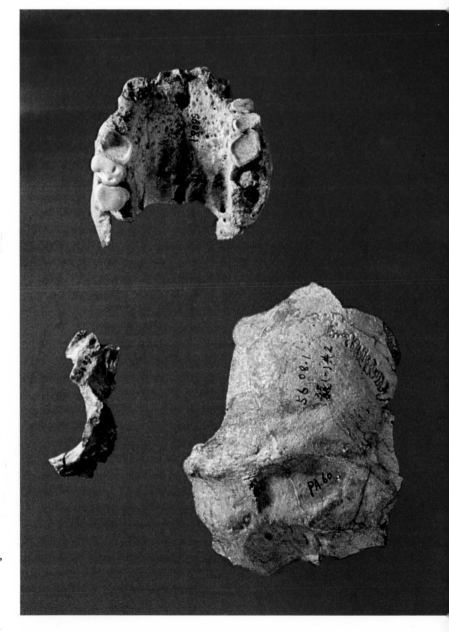

Skull fragments of Qilinshan Man. (59 mm, 46.2 mm, 103.2 mm) (E109°05′, N23°40′)

Duleyan Man

Fossil human tooth from Duleyan (occlusal view). (E109°20′, N24°15′)

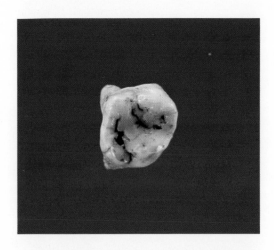

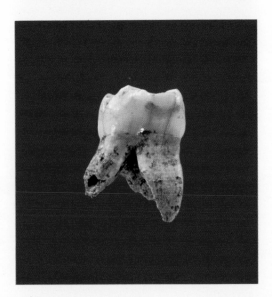

Fossil human tooth from Duleyan (lateral view).

In Duleyan village, twelve kilometers southwest of Liuzhou City in the Guangxi Zhuang Autonomous Region are the Duleyan lava caves in which are travertine sediments well-developed and moulded into spectacular shapes. Caves open to visitors are Panlong Cave, Tongtian Cave and Shuiyun Cave which yielded the fossils. Apart from Neoanthropic fossil tooth, fossils of *Ursus* sp. (bear), *Arctonyx* cf. *rostratus* (badger), *Canis* sp., *Equus* sp. (horse), *Cervus* sp. (deer), and *Sus* sp. (pig) were also found. The deposit is supposed to be of late Pleistocene.

Bailiandong Cave, Liuzhou (Liuchou)

Since liberation in 1949, investigations have been constantly carried out in the Guangxi Zhuang Autonomous Region into Quaternary mammals, human fossils and paleocultures. Stone artifacts were found in a number of caves, along with Neolithic Age relics, e.g. polished stone axes and earthenware fragments. But in the deposit of several caves such as Bailiandon Cave of Liuzhou City and Aidong Cave of Chongzuo County, only stone artifacts and no relics of a later period were discovered. These stone artifacts were mostly made from pebbles showing rather crude workmanship. Distinction could hardly be made between these artifacts and the local Neolithic Age artifacts in type and manufacture. Since no remains of a later period were discovered, researchers who studied the artifacts believe that the paleolithic stone implements in the caves in Guangxi may belong to late Pleistocene, i.e. late Old Stone Age.

Stone artifacts from Bailiandong Cave and elsewhere. (95 mm, 105 mm) (E109°20′, N24°15′)

Shangsong, Baise

In 1973 stone artifacts were found in the third terrace (35 meters above river water level) by the Youjiang River 300 meters southwest of Shangsongcun Village about 11 kilometers west of the Baise County seat in the Guangxi Zhuang Autonomous Region. The implements, shaped out of heavy pebbles, were mostly crude choppers. Researchers have determined that they are different to a certain extent from the paleolithic stone artifacts of the same period in other provinces, but have affinities with those found in local caves. Since only a few stone artifacts have been collected and no fossils of any kind were found in association, this site is tentatively classified, according to geomorphology and the stone artifacts, as late Paleolithic Age. The possibility of its belonging to a later period is not precluded.

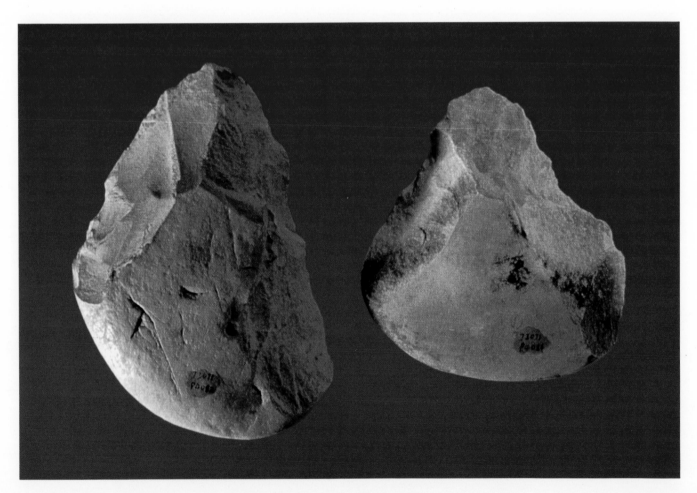

Choppers from Shangsong, Baise County. (182 mm, 138 mm) (E106°25′, N23°55′)

Ziyang (Tzeyang) Man

When the Chengdu-Chongqing Railway was under construction in 1951, railway workers found Ziyang Man's fossil remains by the Huangshanxi Creek in Ziyang County, Sichuan Province. The fossils were a cranium with its base missing, and a maxilla. They were ascertained to be part of the skull of a neoanthropic female of over 50.

Found along with Ziyang Man fossil remains were many animal fossils such as *Arctonyx* (badger), *Hyaena, Felis tigris* (tiger), *Hystrix* (porcupine), *Rhizomy* (bamboo rat), *Equus* sp. (horses), *Rhinoceros* cf. *sinensis, Muntiacus, Rusa* (deer), *Bibos gaurus* (bison), *Stegodon orientalis* (elephant)—all late Pleistocene species. Apart from these, in a layer of coarse sand and small pebbles was a rare find—an awl with a short and blunt head made of a triangular-shaped bone by scraping.

Ziyang (Tzeyang) Man site. (E104°30′, N30°10′)

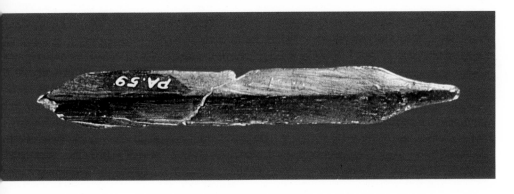

Bone awl of Ziyang Man. (105 mm)

Skull of Ziyang Man (lateral view). (170 mm)

Fulin, Hanyuan

A site yielding Paleolithic Age cultural relics was discovered in 1960 at Fulin Townlet in Hanyuan County, Sichuan Province. Systematic excavations were carried out in 1972, bringing to light over 5,000 paleolithic stone artifacts, abundant traces of the use of fire, a small number of mammalian and *palecypoda* (shell) fossils, many prints of tree leaves, chiefly those of the chestnut tree. The stone artifacts were small in size, most of them being 2—3cm-long stone flakes, cores and tools. Compared with those discovered at other sites in China of the same period, the average size of the stone artifacts found in Fulin approximates that of the stone artifacts discovered at Salawusu, but smaller than elsewhere. This feature has led to naming them "Fulin Culture", a culture of the late Paleolithic Age.

Stone tools from Fulin site in Hanyuan County. (22 mm, 21 mm, 28 mm)

Scrapers from Fulin site. (32 mm, 19 mm, 38 mm)

Fulin site.

Banqiao, Lunan

In 1961 paleolithic stone artifacts were discovered in Lunan County (referred to as Yiliang County in the first treatises on this site), Yunnan Province. These artifacts were scattered on the second and third terraces of the Bapanjiang River near Banqiao Village, Lunan County. Among the stone artifacts were long, thin flakes, scrapers and points, mostly stone flake tools. The type and trimming technique were of the style of Paleolithic Age artifacts. Moreover, no Neolithic Age relics were found on the terraces, therefore the stone artifacts discovered near Banqiao Village were considered to be relics from the late Paleolithic Age.

Stone tools from Banjiao and other places in Lunan County. (51 mm, 58 mm, 63 mm) (E103°35′, N24°40′)

Xichou Man

Xichou Man fossil remains were found in Xianrendong Cave in Xichou County in the Wenshan Zhuang-Miao Autonomous Prefecture, Yunnan Province.

The fossil remains consist of five teeth which are close to modern human teeth in shape and have the features of the late Neoanthropic man. Also found with Xichou Man fossil remains were 32 species of animal fossils, including *Myotis* sp. (bat), *Rhizomys* (bamboo rat), *Macaca* (monkey), *Ailuropoda* (giant panda), *Viverricula* (civet), *Crocuta ultima* (hyena), *Stegodon orientalis* (elephant), *Rhinoceros sinensis* and *Rusa* (deer), all common in the late Pleistocene in South China.

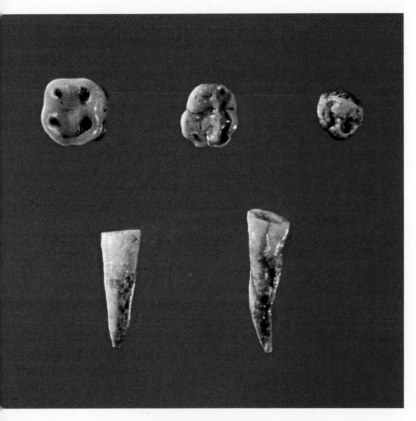

Ailurus fulgeus (lesser panda) and *Viverricula indica* (civet) fossils from Xichou site. (11 mm, 12.4 mm)

Fossil human teeth of Xichou Man. (10.5 mm, 8.3 mm, 9.1 mm, 8.9 mm, 10.8 mm) (E109°25′, N24°22′)

Lijiang (Lichiang) Man

Three thighbones were found in the spring of 1956 at the site of the Mujiaqiao water conservancy project in the Yangxi People's Commune of Lijiang County, Yunnan Province. In March 1964, a human skull fossil was added to the collection.

According to the studies by the Yunnan Provincial Museum, the Lijiang Man skull is that of a young female, and has close affinities with modern man and has Mongoloid features.

The geologic age of the layer possibly yielding Lijiang Man fossils and the symbiotic animal (i.e. Axis (deer)) fossil remains is late Pleistocene.

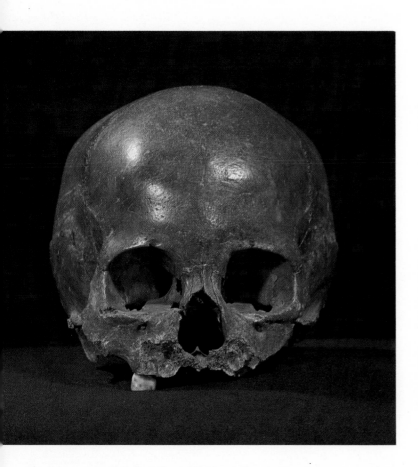

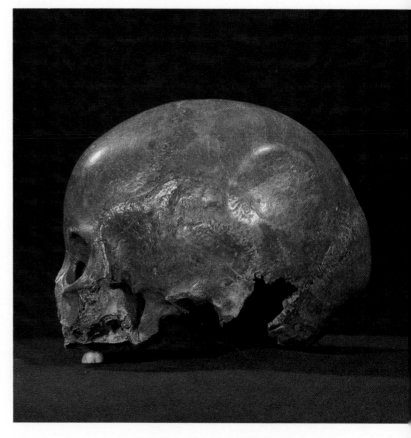

Fossil human skull from Lijiang (Lichiang) County (front view). (141 mm) (E100°20′, N27°05′)

Fossil human skull from Lijiang County (lateral view). (167 mm)

Lijiang site where the human skull was found.

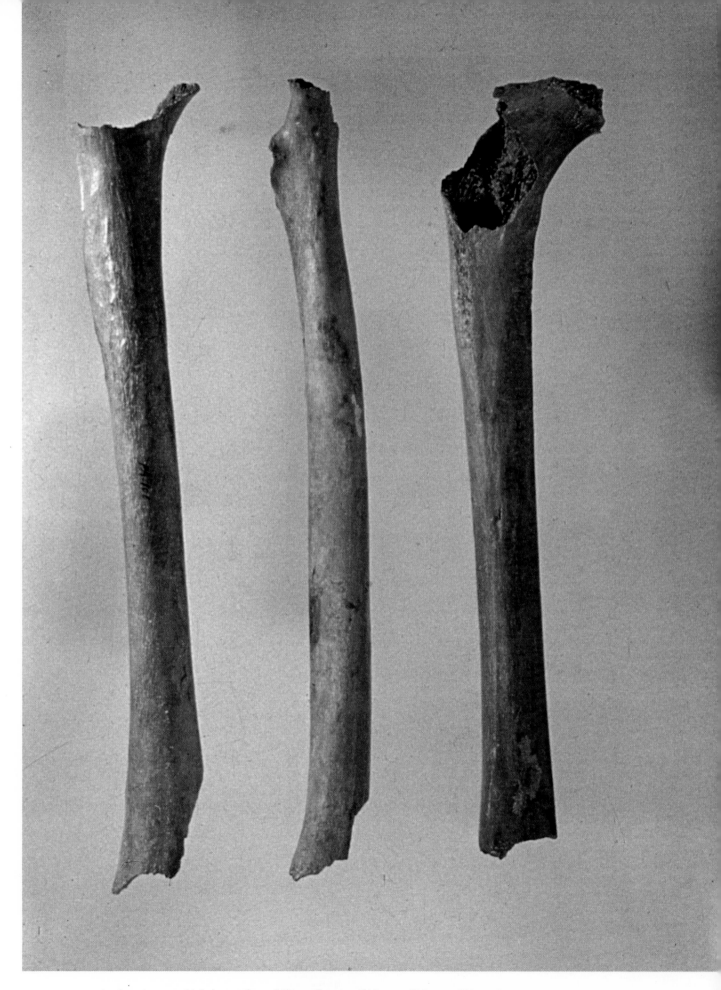

Ancient human thigh bones from Lijiang County. (315 mm, 324 mm, 314 mm)

Xingyi Man

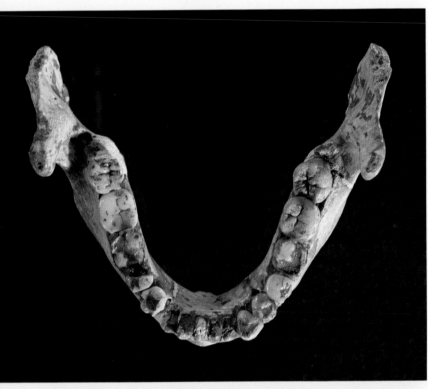

Twenty-five kilometers northeast of the Xingyi County seat, or 350 kilometers from the city of Guiyang, Guizhou Province, is Maomao cave, the mouth of which is 45 meters above the river water level. In 1975 in deposit in the cave were found human fossil remains, more than 5,000 paleolithic stone artifacts and a considerable number of bone tools. The stone artifacts were of a fixed type and fine workmanship. The spearhead-shaped points were the most regular among them. The bone shovels were made of polished deer horn. The sharpened facet of the shovel edge forms a 45° angle, a feature never found before in China. This collection is still under study. It is supposed that they belong to the late Paleolithic epoch. The cultural features found in this site are rare in China. The many human fossil remains, the abundant stone artifacts of fine workmanship and the numerous bone tools found at the same site not only rank this discovery first among sites of the late Paleolithic Age found in South China but also give the site a prominent position across the whole land.

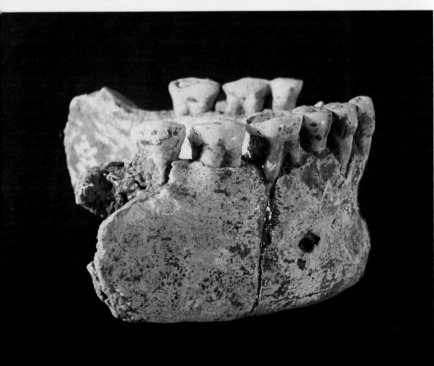

Mandible (lower jaw bone) of Xinyi Man. (100 mm) (E105°02′, N25°10′) (occlusal view)

Mandible of Xinyi Man. (91 mm) (lateral view)

Point of Xinyi Man. (55 mm)

Femur (thigh bone) of Xinyi Man. (167 mm)

Points of Xinyi Man. (92 mm, 78 mm)

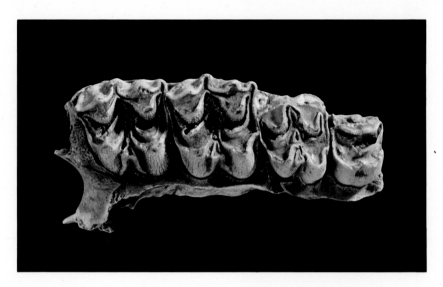

Maxilla (upper jaw bone) of *Rusa* (deer) from Xinyi Man site. (85 mm)

Spades made of antler of deer from Xinyi Man site. (156 mm, 113 mm)

Tooth of *Ursus kokeni* (bear) from Xinyi Man site. (35 mm)

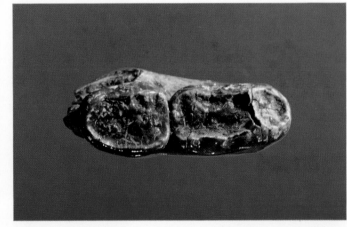

Jiangsu – Zhejiang – Shandong

Fragmentary fossil remains of primitive man were found in the provinces of Jiangsu, Zhejiang and Shandong. (1) Jiande Man discovered in Jiande County, Zhejiang Province: In winter 1974, in the upper fossil-bearing layer of Wugui Cave in the Shangxinqiao production brigade, Lijia People's Commune, a highly fossilized human upper canine was found, which bore close resemblance to the canine of Lijiang (Likiang) Man. The tooth belonged to a neoanthropic male of about 30 years of age. (2) Xiacaowan Man discovered in Sihong County, Jiangsu Province: In June 1954, a fragment of human femur was found on the river bank of Xiacaowan. Unlike the femur of modern man which curves forward, it resembled that of Peking Man. Its bone wall was thin and the marrow cavity large, approximating that of the Upper Cave Man. Since no other fossils were found, Xiacaowan Man was tentatively classified under Neoanthropic stage. (3) Wuzhutai Man discovered in Xintai County, Shandong Province: A human tooth was found in a cave at Wuzhutai in April 1966. It was the first or second molar of a young female. Morphologically it was more developed than that of Peking Man and approximated that of the modern man.

Jiande

Fossil human canine from Wuguidong Cave, Jiande County.
(9.5 mm) (E119°02′, N29°15′)

Fossil human canine from
Wuguidong Cave.

Xintai

Fossil human molar found near Wuzhutai Village, Xintai County, Shandong (Shantung) Province. (10.3 mm) (E117°45′, N35°55′)

Fossil human femur (thigh bone) fragment from Xiacaowan, Sihong County. (152.7 mm) (E118°10′, N33°25′)

Xiacaowan

Paleolithic stone artifacts were found in a cave in Shandong Province in 1965. These artifacts were buried in a layer of sandy clay which could be subdivided into an upper and lower culture layer. A total of 38 stone artifacts were obtained in addition to a small number of fossil remains of mammals such as *Equus caballus* (horse) and *Equus hemionus* (donkey). There were both thick and thin flakes. The only type of stone tools was scrapers of which the thicker ones were to some extent typical. The geologic age may be late Paleolithic Age.

A Cave in Shandong

Stone tools from Shandongyidong. (47 mm, 48 mm, 41 mm, 31 mm) (E118°15′, N35°05′)

Zuozhen Man, Taiwan

Taiwan Province, an inalienable part of Chinese territory, was connected to the mainland with a land bridge in the Quaternary period. Human fossils and paleolithic stone artifacts recovered in Taiwan testify that during the Quaternary period ancestors of the Chinese nation came to live, labor and multiply on this treasure island.

Zuozhen Man: It has been reported that a human fossil was picked up at Cailiaoxi Creek in Tainan County, Taiwan Province. This fossil, a part of the parietal bone, could be that of a Neoanthropic man living 30,000 years ago. Analysis of the available geologic data shows that during the late glacial epoch in the later part of the Pleistocene epoch the sea subsided, leaving the island of Taiwan connected to the mainland. It is probable that in this period Zuozhen Man moved overland from the mainland to Taiwan.

Paleolithic stone artifacts at Baxiangudong Cave cluster: It has been reported that Paleolithic stone artifacts were uncovered in five caves in the Baxiangudong Cave cluster at Zhangyuancun Village in Taidong County. Carbon-14 dating of one cave gave a reading of about 15,000 years.

THE FOSSIL APES

Abundant ape fossils were discovered in southern China after liberation. These fossils, though debatable as to their position in the system, are of importance to investigations into the origin of man. Fossils of apes are thus included here to show the advances which Chinese paleoanthropologists have made in the study of these creatures. These fossils offer valuable scientific data for research into the origin of man and the evolution of advanced Primates.

Ramapithecus lufengensis: *Ramapithecus lufengensis* was discovered in a Pliocene stratum in a coal pit at Shihuiba in Lufeng County, Yunnan Province. Excavations in 1975 and 1976 brought to light two fairly complete lower jawbones of ape and over 100 teeth. These lower jawbones represent two types of apes. The one discovered in 1975 belongs to the type of *Sivapithecus* and was most likely the ancestor of the orang-utan; the other discovered in 1976 represents *Ramapithecus,* a transitional type from ape to man. Found along with the *Ramapithecus* were large numbers of *Hipparion* (three-toed horse) fossils.

Dryopithecus keiyuanensis: In February 1956, members of the Southwest China Bureau of Geology found five teeth in a Tertiary lignite deposit at Xiaolongtan, Kaiyuan County, Yunnan Province. These were teeth of a lower jaw of a female individual. In early 1957 another five teeth discovered in the same lignite deposit were presented to our institute by the Yunnan Provincial Museum. They belonged to a male individual.

Gigantopithecus: The Gigantopithecus came to be known to paleoanthropologists in 1935. The fossils were without context as they were obtained from a traditional Chinese apothecary in Hong Kong. After liberation, at the end of 1955, researchers were dispatched to the Guangxi Zhuang Autonomous Region to search for remains of the *Gigantopithecus*. In early 1956 three teeth (M_1, P_1 and M^1) were dug up from a purple argillaceous deposit in Heidong Cave at Daxin County. This provided a clue to the location and the stratum. Large-scale investigations were carried out in the winter of 1956 in Guangxi. In addition to some teeth of the *Gigantopithecus* found at Wuming, Lipu and other places in Guangxi, a *Gigantopithecus* cave was found in Lengzhaishan Hill at Liucheng County with the help of the local people. Excavations over several years brought to light three complete lower jawbones, over a thousand teeth and abundant mammalian fossils. In 1965 twelve *Gigantopithecus* teeth were found in a cave at Wuming; in 1970 nine *Gigantopithecus* teeth were found at Jianshi, Hubei Province. The other animal fossils collected from the above-mentioned sites prove that the *Gigantopithecus* lived between early and middle Pleistocene.

The *Australopithecus* and the *Gigantopithecus* of West Hubei: In Longdong Cave, Gaoping, at Jianshi County, Hubei Province, three advanced Primate tooth fossils were discovered in 1970 in the same stratum where the teeth of the *Gigantopithecus* were found. A lower first molar was found at Badong County, Hubei Province. Researchers who reported these specimens ascertained that morphologically these teeth resembled the molars of the *Australopithecus* and are therefore the first fossils of the *Australopithecus* ever found in China. According to a study of the mammalian fossils discovered in the same stratum the geologic age is slightly later than the *Gigantopithecus* cave at Liucheng County, possibly of the later part of the early Pleistocene.

The discoveries of these fossil remains of apes afford fresh scientific data for research into the time and distribution with regard to the origin of man.

Ramapithecus lufengensis

A distant view of *Ramapithecus lufengensis* site, Lufeng County. (E102°05′, N25°10′)

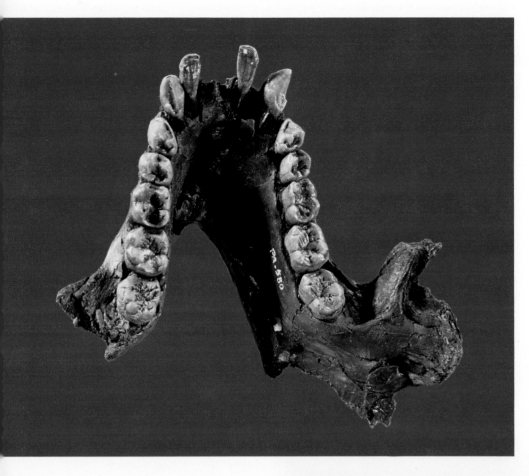

Mandible (lower jaw bone) of *Ramapithecus lufen-gensis* (occlusal view). (96.5 mm)

Mandible (lower jaw bone) of *Sivapithecus yunnanensis* (occlusal view). (66 mm)

Dryopithecus keiyuanensis

A distant view of *Dryopithecus keiyuanensis* site in Xiaolongtan coalmine, Kaiyuan County. (E103°25′, N23°40′)

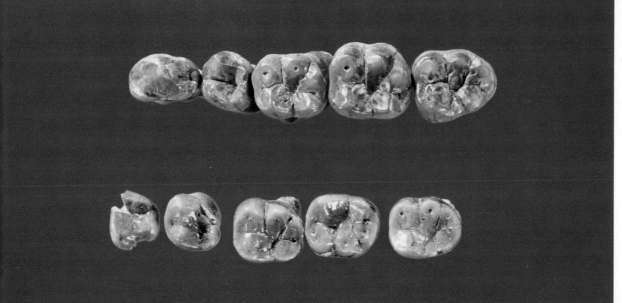

Teeth of *Dryopithecus keiyuanensis* (occlusal view). (58.2 mm)

167

Gigantopithecus in Liucheng

Mandibles (lower jaw bone) of *Gigantopithecus blacki* from Liucheng County. (occlusal view) (91 mm, 102 mm, 148 mm)

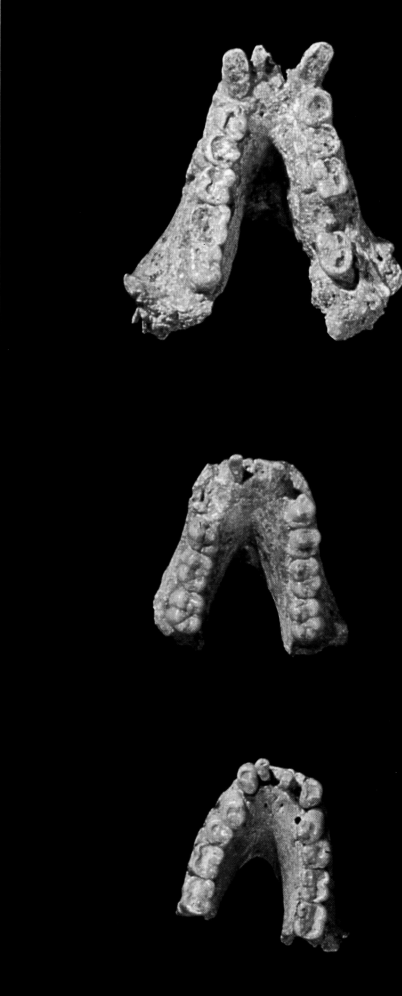

◁A distant view of *Gigantopithecus* Cave in Liucheng County. (E109°15′, N24°10′)

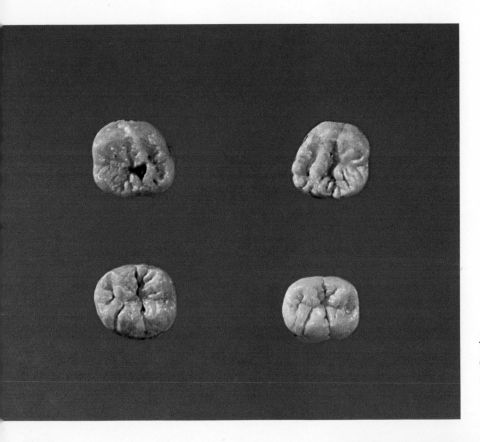

Teeth of *Australopithecus* from western Hubei (occlusal view). (12.2 mm, 13.6 mm, 14.1 mm, 14.0 mm) (E110°04′, N30°38′)

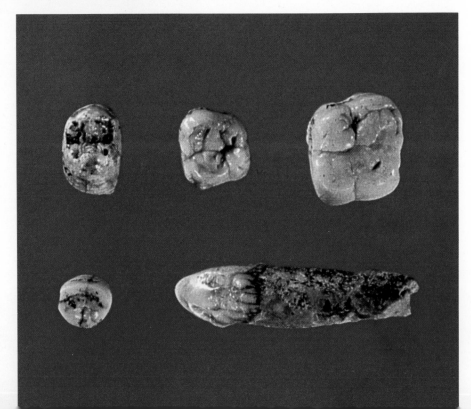

Teeth of *Gigantopithecus blacki* from western Hubei (occlusal view).

170

Australopithecus and *Gigantopithecus* site in Jianshi County, Hubei.

Gigantopithecus in Wuming

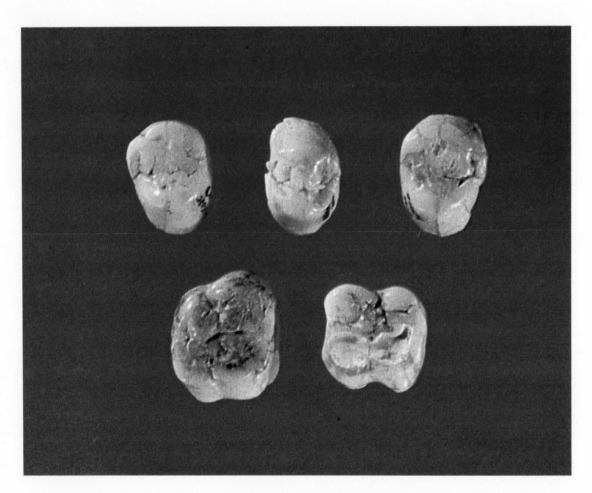

Gigantopithecus teeth from Wuming County (occlusal view). (E108°15′, N22°59′)

Gigantopithecus Cave of Wuming. ▷

POSTSCRIPT

This book aims to provide readers with an overall view of the academic achievements of Chinese paleoanthropology up to the end of 1976. The explanatory notes to each site were written mainly on the basis of relevant works published before the end of 1976. In most cases the notes incorporated the main conclusions of the published works; only in isolated cases were slight alterations made. Some of the data in this book are published here for the first time, part of them are new research results. In the notes to one or two older sites, new data are also included.

This book contains photographs of human fossils, paleolithic stone artifacts, bone implements, ornaments, traces of the use of fire as well as fossils of some mammals typical of the time. To make the book more interesting and readable and give the reader some general ideas about early primitive society and its natural surroundings, this book has included paintings depicting the primitive man's life and work, drawings of reconstructed ancient animals and pictures of animals and plants belonging to the same genera as the extint animals and plants, or pictures of closely related species.

For readers interested in the geographical locations of the fossil sites, a map has been provided at the beginning of the book showing the distribution of the major sites of human fossils, paleolithic artifacts and fossils of the apes in China. The longitude and latitude of each site are given in the caption after the first of the pictures of the site.

Lengths of the major finds are given in the captions to provide readers an idea of the size. In view of the variety of the finds, measurements are made in the following ways:

1. The measurement of human fossils: The frontal view of the skull gives the breadth of the skull. The side view gives the length of the skull. The mandibular occlusal view gives the overall length. The dental occlusal view of the incisor gives the mesiodistal diameter.

2. In the cases of stone flakes, the length means the projecting length of two extreme points of the specimen on a straight line passing through striking point and consistent with the direction of striking force; the length of a stone core is measured in the same way on the main working surface; the same applies to stone implements.

3. The measurement of animal fossils: The way to measure an animal skull is the same as used for that of the human skull. The length of lower jawbone is the distance between the incisor to the posterior end of the fossil. The length of a tooth is the mesiodistal diameter.

This book was compiled collectively by Chang Senshui, Gu Yumin, Bao Yixin, Shen Wenlong, Wang Zhefu, Wang Chunde and Du Zhi of the compiling group organized by the Institute of Vertebrate Paleontology and Paleoanthropology of the Chinese Academy of Sciences.

We wish to express our gratitude here to the late President of the Chinese Academy of Sciences, Guo Moruo, who had given us great encouragement in our work and who had kindly written the inscription to the book. We wish also to thank the staff members in various departments of our institute. We are indebted to the Institute of Botany of the Chinese Academy of Sciences, the Institute of Archeology of the Chinese Academy of Social Sciences, the Museum of Chinese History, the Beijing Museum of Natural History, the Beijing Zoo, the Zhengzhou Museum as well as related departments in the provinces of Liaoning, Guizhou, Gansu and Shandong, the Guangxi Zhuang Autonomous Region and the Ningxia Hui Autonomous Region for their active cooperation and generous assistance.

CONTENTS

DISTRIBUTION OF PRIMITIVE MAN IN CHINA

Urümqi

Lanzhou

Chengdu

Lhasa

LEGEND

◯ Site of Protoanthropic Stage

⊖ Site of Paleoanthropic Stage

⊘ Site of Neoanthropic Stage

⊕ Site of Fossil Ape

Kunming